FEMINISM IN
AMERICAN
POLITICS

Copublished with the
Eagleton Institute of Politics,
Rutgers University

FEMINISM IN AMERICAN POLITICS

A Study of Ideological Influence

Claire Knoche Fulenwider

American Political Parties
and Elections

general editor:
Gerald M. Pomper

PRAEGER

PRAEGER SPECIAL STUDIES • PRAEGER SCIENTIFIC

Library of Congress Cataloging in Publication Data

Fulenwider, Claire Knoche.
    Feminism in American politics.

    (American political parties and elections)
    Bibliography: p.
    Includes index.
    1. Feminism--United States. 2. Women in politics--
United States. I. Title. II. Series.
HQ1426.F88   301.41'2'0973   79-25131
ISBN 0-03-053461-5

Published in 1980 by Praeger Publishers
CBS Educational and Professional Publishing
A Division of CBS, Inc.
521 Fifth Avenue, New York, New York 10017 U.S.A.

© 1980 by Praeger Publishers

0123456789   038   987654321

Printed in the United States of America

To Hood, the college that made a difference for me and many other women,

To the women who have made my life different and better:
Mom
Marie
Dolly
Gigi
Sandra
Gina
Barbara
Maureen
Kay
Cathy
Gudren
Marlee
Linda
Karen
Donna
Robin
Karla
and Arlene,

And to Nina and Nathan—in the hope that for them it *will* be different.

PREFACE

*A*dults of both sexes and all ages are consciously, and often alarmingly, aware of great changes in U.S. social and political life. A peanut farmer is president. The rate of inflation seems fixed in double digits. After years of nonrecognition of the People's Republic of China, there are warm, frequent, and almost countless exchange programs between that nation and ours. Americans who never thought twice about driving anywhere are suddenly making millionaires out of bicycle manufacturers. Egypt and Israel have signed a peace treaty and SALT II has been negotiated between the United States and Soviet Union; yet threats of nuclear power plant accidents have heightened Americans' concern with holocausts far closer to home. Social change in U.S. life seems ubiquitous and profound.

One of the clearest indicators of the depths of such change is the rapid alteration of the roles and attitudes of U.S. women. In unprecedented numbers, women are entering the work force, postponing childbirth, and opting against marriage. At the local level, the number of female political candidates is increasing at the same time that the Equal Rights Amendment is being sandbagged by the new far right and Phyllis Schlafly's Eagle Forum.

A question constantly posed by social scientists, of course, is, To what extent do such social changes influence the political system? Do social forces leave political behavior virtually unchanged or do they significantly modify citizen demands and system response?

Long-standing debate exists within political science over whether ideas, either new or old, result in changes in political behavior. Many scholars have voiced skepticism over the rational consistency of the electorate. Others have scorned the system's capacity to change. To the extent that either is true, hopes for serious reform are dimmed.

My own view is less bleak. I was raised in a household where my grandfather, who had been mayor of Baltimore some 25 years before my appearance, was a living indicator of system responsiveness. In my adult years, I have observed most people I know giving serious thought to their evaluation of candidates' character and ability as well as issue position. I believe most people have some principles, at least, upon which they take consistent stands. I believe feminists tend to do this to a greater extent than does the average citizen, man or woman. I also believe the women's movement is a far more powerful force for social change in contemporary U.S. life than most people acknowledge. But we don't know that these beliefs are realistic—hence, this research effort.

The import of this work, thus the audience to which it is addressed, is broad. First, I hope practitioners and students of political science will find these chapters informative. Citizens' political behavior is cued substantially by the ideas in which they believe, according to these findings, and feminism proves to be a belief set or ideology of considerable political significance. Second, this book is addressed to all women and men in the general public concerned with and in some way committed to the women's movement. For supporters discouraged by the slowness of feminist success on various fronts, I hope this work will encourage them both to take heart and to muster greater patience and perseverance. Feminism is making a difference politically—among political attitudes and, to a lesser extent, political behavior.

In addition, this book is aimed at the political leadership of this country, its message being that women's relations to the political system are changing. Women are becoming angrier and more aware. They are, consequently, starting to act differently politically. Demands by women for substantive and not merely symbolic equality are not likely soon to diminish. Thus, lastly, these findings speak to the leadership of all segments of the women's movement, to tell them that their efforts have not been in vain. The silence that has often greeted much of their activity and rhetoric reflects a quiet surface that masks profound impacts. The fight may not have been won, but it certainly has not been lost. A significant portion of the U.S. populace is responding to feminist ideas and changing because of them.

While the conclusions of this work and any flaws in its logic, prose, or methodology can be attributed only to me, both the research itself and the intellectual questions that led to that research benefited from the serious contributions of many people. Jack Dennis, more than any other colleague, has read repeated drafts, encouraged, and criticized constructively. Barbara Hinckley, Gina Sapiro, and Murray Edelman all read and advised me on earlier drafts and encouraged me to seek publication. Dick Merelman originally aroused my curiosity about the relationship between ideology and behavior. Numerous women, organizations, and experiences reinforced my interest in the women's movement. The graduate women in the political science department at the University of Wisconsin-Madison, provided support and positive feedback at numerous points in the process. The Data and Computer Center of the Madison Academic Computing Center gave crucial assistance with data access, file management, programming consultation, and the like. June Harrington and Alice Brown typed ably. Jerry Knoche endured and encouraged. Colleagues in the Women's Studies Program at the University of Wisconsin-Madison and especially at the Wisconsin Center for Public Policy consistently maintained my morale through a difficult year. My friends and family added pleasure and generally cheer to the overall process and my editor, Gerald Pomper, added valuable suggestions and criticisms. My deep thanks go to all of these people.

CONTENTS

LIST OF TABLES

LIST OF FIGURES

FEMINISM IN
AMERICAN
POLITICS

1

IDEOLOGY AND
SOCIAL CHANGE

"There ain't no buckin' the system. Each year the gov'ment takes more and more from ya. I even stopped workin' overtime last year because it can't pay no more. Puts me in another tax bracket and the gov'ment takes so much then that I'm only gettin' a buck thirty-six an hour. So I don't work the overtime anymore. No matter what you do, they'll get it out of you some way. You're not gonna change the system."   (meat-cutter)

"You know, the only ones gettin' a decent shake these days are broads and jungle bunnies. They've got the government scared to death of law suits. Those guys runnin' things want to stay right where they are—in the power and in the bucks. More and more it's two classes in this country— the rich and the poor. They try to make you think you're not poor, but compared to them, we are. Now they're lettin' blacks and women get a little bigger share and tryin' to make us all think it's a fair share. I don't know, though, I guess the government'll keep them where they want them, too."   (retired railroad worker)

"It's hard to say. All I know is, they got more chance than you or me because they're together and angry and the gov'ment knows it. Guys like you and me are on our own and the gov'ment just ignores us."[1]
                                                        (meat-cutter)

*P*olitics—who gets what, when and how—poses questions that demand answers of ordinary citizens and social scientists alike. Although vocabulary and style of speech may differ, social scientists might find, were they to compare notes with the people on the street, that the two groups agree more often than either would suspect. For example, one inference to be drawn from the meat-cutter's remarks is that a social group that is "together" will be better able to effect political change than one that is not. He may not be too far from right, for substantial evidence suggests that most political reforms in the United States have been closely tied to organized movements, movements whose two characteristic traits were the possession of a clear political ideology and the forceful expression of political demands.[2] As our meat-cutter might express this, such movements "have it together." They are able to affect the distribution of social benefits, to influence the political processes that determine who gets what, when and why.[3]

Social movements act by politicizing various forms of conflict—economic, social, racial. They articulate dissatisfaction with the existing social order and consciously aim to bring about social change, usually succeeding in at least some measure.[4]

Yet political science research has often tended to focus more upon political stability than upon the processes of political change. The meat-cutter's hunch has rarely been pursued. This study, the purpose of which is to investigate a contemporary social movement (feminism) and its influence upon the political attitudes and behavior of the U.S. electorate, tests that hunch, asking whether a movement's ideology is central in promoting political change.

But are social movements related to political change? Why is a study of ideology helpful to an understanding of this relationship? To answer these questions we need first to look at the concept of a social movement and then at the role of ideology within such a movement.

SOCIAL MOVEMENTS AND POLITICAL CHANGE

While the concept of a social movement has been defined in various ways, the definition that guides this study (also see Chapter 2) is the notion that a social movement expresses a widely shared set of attitudes and actions consciously held and pursued by a large group of people and aimed toward causing structural and ideological change within the society.[5] Change of this extent is often a realistic objective, since social movements tend to clarify issues, heighten public awareness of social problems, and serve as a focal point for the political unrest of numerous citizens. Movements raise society's consciousness to claims of injustice from groups that have previously been ignored or that perceive themselves as seriously deprived of social rewards to which they are justly due.

In addition, social movements accomplish certain objectives for movement supporters. Participation is a movement increases the sensitivity of those involved to inequities to which they have been subjected. Political activity clearly aimed at a specific goal both focuses personal unrest and contributes to a sense of personal effectiveness, of expending effort toward a worthwhile end. As movement supporters come to recognize shared concerns between themselves and others, social movement leaders hope and expect that such individuals will cluster about the movement, expanding its membership, if not its active core. Shared dissatisfaction and unrest be it with the weather or with the distribution of social benefits, may spawn a strange but growing array of allies; and movement growth is important if a movement's legitimacy and power are to be sufficient to move the larger and more ponderous political system.[6]

Social movements aim to change the social and political system.[7] The medium they use for triggering political change, however, is personal. Social movements motivate large sectors of the populace to act loudly and clearly enough that their demands are both heard and responded to. The ends social movements pursue are systemic: institutional and structural change. The means to those ends, however, are individual: personal attitudinal and behavioral change on a large scale.

Political change, then, has two obvious and interacting faces: the personal, individual side, in which segments of the masses respond, demand, and act to bring about change; and the systemic side, in which the political system itself responds, refuses to respond, or fails. This study focuses on the former face of the change process—the personal, individual dimension.

POLITICAL IDEOLOGY AND SOCIAL CHANGE

Personal acceptance of a movement's ideology by members of the political system establishes a support base for movement demands. But acceptance of a new or modified political ideology on a large scale is a complex process. Many persons need to perceive political reality in a way different from the norm. Major components of the prevalent status quo need to be questioned and rejected. New possibilities for the social order need to be grasped and desired. A clear political ideology, while central to a social movement's effectiveness, is difficult to achieve.

A social movement's ideology fails if it garners only intellectual support among movement followers. Ideology needs to evoke commitment that propels believers to action. A social movement ideology, feminist ideology being a clear case in point, aims for change—change in personal attitudes and behavior, change in the system. In short, feminist ideology, like other social movement ideologies, aims at both sides of the coin of political change—the personal and the systemic. As Freeman (1975a, p. 5) argues:

> . . . a successful movement provides an *intersection* between personal and social change. Personal changes can be a vehicle to more concrete

social changes, and are also often a result; but if a movement restricts itself to change purely on the personal level its impact on society remains minimal. It is only when private disputes that result from personal changes are translated into public demands that a movement enters the political arena and can make use of political institutions to reach its goals of social change.

Ideology acts as a catalyst to enhance the breadth and the intensity of demands for social change. Widespread acceptance of a movement's ideology helps propel the movement into the political arena and guarantees a hearing of, if not a positive answer for, movement demands. Such acceptance results from clear evidence of strong links between support for a movement's ideology and political activity of movement supporters within the political system. In other words, the system grants legitimacy to movement demands when people are willing to act on their beliefs, when believing a certain ideology actually makes a difference in what people do.

How ideology relates to the way people think and act has long been a central question for political science.[8] Empirical investigations of this relationship, however, have occurred only recently. Converse (1964) explored the relationship between national political ideology and political attitudes. Ashford (1972) investigated the relationship between political ideology and mass political participation in several nations. Putnam (1973) studied the relation between elite ideology and legislative politics. Now this study looks at the influence of ideology upon political attitudes and behavior of the mass electorate.

Political change is the broad focus of the study, with the personal rather than the systemic perspective of change being addressed here. Rather than focusing upon how women differ from men in their political attitudes and behavior, or upon gender and role differences in this area, as most other recent research on women and politics has done, this study focuses upon feminist ideology and the political phenomena that can be traced to it. Specifically, five basic questions are investigated to explore the nature of the relationship between political ideology and political behavior: How is feminism structured as a political ideology? Is the nature of support for feminist ideology different for men than for women? How does feminism influence the political attitudes of its supporters? What influence does feminism have upon the political behavior of women? Finally, how does race affect each of these relationships?

In effect, this research asks whether one's being a feminist makes any difference, politically. It attempts to answer questions such as the following: Are women who support the current women's movement different in any politically significant ways from women who do not support the movement? What trends are evident in this support? What changes in the relation of women to the body politic do these trends and relationships portend? In short, what personal political impact are the ideas of the women's movement actually having "out there" among typical American women?

The literature and the data base available for such a study are rich. There is now a broad base of primary feminist writings—one far more extensive than was available for the study of the black civil rights or black power movement, the student protest movement, or the antiwar movement of the 1960s and early 1970s. In addition, a strong data bank exists for quantitative analysis through national electoral surveys that include items for feminism, political attitudes, and political behavior. For this study, cross-sectional national electoral surveys conducted by the Center for Political Studies at the University of Michigan in 1972 and 1976 form the data base.

The relationship between feminist political ideology and the political attitudes and behavior of American women is explored here in several stages. The second chapter analyzes and argues for the extent to which the contemporary women's movement is a social movement, given its history, structure, leadership, goals, and so forth. Whether the ideas of feminism can properly be regarded as a political ideology is dealt with in the third chapter. There, ideological differences within the women's movement are clarified and commonalities of thought stressed. A strong argument is made that feminism is, indeed, a political ideology.

The empirical analysis of feminism as a political ideology begins in Chapter 4. The feminism index used for statistical analysis throughout the quantitative sections of the study is presented and conceptually related to feminist ideology. Feminism is also analyzed in this chapter to examine how closely it resembles an ideology in content, structure, and function.

Chapter 5 presents findings that show feminism differs in several important ways depending upon whether the feminist is male or female. Clear differences are found in the content of feminism, its cognitive structure, its demographic correlates, and its psychological associations, depending upon the sex of the believer. (Changes in the extent and composition of support for the women's movement in the 1970s are presented here as well.)

The relationship between feminism, political attitudes, and race is explored in Chapter 6. Specifically, two broad categories of political attitudes are investigated: personal political attitudes that center upon the individual's perceptions of her or his ability, responsibility, and desire to interact with the political system; and system-focused political attitudes that deal with the individual's perceptions of the government. In this part of the study the sample of women is partitioned on the basis of race and three primary analyses are performed: (1) changes in the association of feminism with political attitudes between groups (divided according to race); (2) differences in the means of political attitudes between the groups; and (3) differences in the relationship of feminism to the political attitudes of white and minority women. Race strongly compounds feminism's effects.

The final relationship investigated in the study, of course, is that between ideology and political behavior. Chapter 7 tests the relationship of feminism to various forms of political participation and compares these on the basis of race. Differences in levels of participation in the several types of participation, as well as differences in the relationships between feminism and these participation forms, are presented. Here, too, race makes a strong difference.

The final chapter discusses the overall conclusions of the study and its broad implications for political research dealing with mass political behavior, women, social movements, ideology, and political change. Projections of what these data portend for the political behavior of women in the future are offered, particularly as race differences may lead to differences in possible future political behavior.

Feminism makes far-reaching demands for change both upon the political system and upon the traditional attitudes and behaviors of women. Possibilities for change in the political attitudes and activity of the female half of the electorate are profound. This study explores the extent to which such personal political changes are occurring among American women and how strongly influenced these changes have been by belief in feminist political ideology.

Maybe women will get their fair share and maybe they will not. That implied question of the retired railroad worker is not directly answered by this study. Only the political system, women, and other research can hope to determine that. What this study *does* make clear, however, is how widespread feminist attitudes are among American voters and how these beliefs are affecting the political attitudes and behavior of American women.

NOTES

1. A conversation overheard between two white males on a fishing boat off the Virginia coast, June 22, 1978.

2. For extended discussions of the relationship between social movements and political change see Etzioni and Etzioni (1964); Nordskog (1954); Ash (1972); Heberle (1951).

3. This definition of politics, of course, is Harold Lasswell's (1950).

4. Heberle (1951), for instance, argues convincingly that great changes in the social order of states and even continents over the past two centuries are largely the result of social movements. He does not, therefore, argue that most (or even, necessarily, any) social movements achieve all of their goals. But he does argue that most social movements achieve at least some of their goals and that part of a movement's ideology and program demands is usually accepted and eventually assimilated into the existing social-political order.

5. Ash (1972, p. 1). See other related definitions in Von Stein (1964, pp. 81-83); Mc-Laughlin (1969); Heberle (1951, pp. 4-5); Gusfield (1971); Davis (1930); Cantril (1941); Toch (1965); Ash (1972); and Roberts and Kloss (1974).

6. See, especially, Lipsky (1968) for a trenchant discussion of the process of expanding support for grievances by mobilizing the sympathies of third parties and expanding the support

base and, thus, the popular legitimacy of movement demands. Schattschneider's description (1960) of the essential democratic process of socializing conflict is also quite relevant here.

7. By no means, however, do social movements necessarily result in political change. Political change has multiple causes and multiple stages. It is rarely a simple linear process. Change is grounded in dissatisfaction with the status quo, but requires a focus for the dissatisfaction through specific political demands and policy requests. In turn, such demands need the political clout that results from their being pursued with relative intensity and by large numbers of people. Ultimately, of course, for change to occur, demands need to be addressed by the political system in some significant way. Change in components of the political system, in its structure, or in the distribution of its rewards must be sufficiently great that the dissatisfaction is addressed and some large part of the demands actually met. At that point, and only at that point, can substantive political change be said to have occurred.

8. Basic research questions raised by this literature are discussed at some length in the second chapter of Knoche (1978).

2

FEMINISM AS A SOCIAL MOVEMENT

When a social movement is young, changing, and still in its formative stages, analysts seldom speak of it with one voice. Such is certainly the case with the current feminist movement. Both the extent to which feminism is a social movement and the question of whether feminism possesses an ideology are subjects of controversy to contemporary scholars. The first is the subject of this chapter; the second, the subject of the next.

Is feminism a social movement in the social science as contrasted to the popular sense of the term? Is it a strong, effective instrument for social change? Or is the current women's movement more likely a short-lived aberration from traditional role expectations for women?

Answers to these questions run the proverbial gamut. Scholars Helen Dudar (1971) and Barbara Polk (1972) see the current women's movement as closer to a fad than a movement. Amitai Etzioni (1972), on the other hand, sees feminism as a clearly established social movement.

Controversies also exist over the question of whether feminism contains a political ideology, and the two debates are integrally related. Scholars agree that before collective behavior may properly be termed a social movement, a clearly articulated ideology must be present. Thus, agreement on an ideology would establish one major criterion in support of the argument that the women's movement of today is a social movement.

Defining a social movement is far more complex, however, than simply assessing whether a political ideology exists. Social scientists generally agree upon other requisite social movement characteristics as well. Social movements, as differentiated from collective behavior, are usually typified by the following traits: (1) identification with widespread social discontent; (2) a pinpointing of certain social agents, institutions, or policies as the causes of discontent; (3) structure or organization that provides effective communication networks among the discontented for mobilizing action and conveying demands; (4) processes that build support for basic social changes and convey demands for those changes clearly and forcefully; and (5) a clear political ideology.[1]

History has been said to be the graveyard of aristocracies. That may be true. But history is the graveyard of social movements as well. Not, of course, that history is only that, but as history is a record of the demise of powerful groups and collective attempts to become powerful, it is a chronicle of the demise of social movements.

Political systems change—sometimes radically, more often only partially. That change is often the result of the strength of foreign men and weaponry. With even greater frequency, however, rulers are confronted by those from their own nation—the dissatisfied, the women as well as the men, who have come to distrust those currently rich and politically powerful. The feminist movement is one such challenge—a confrontation between existing social structures and the anger and determination of women.

But just what is a social movement, and does the current women's movement qualify as one?

A variety of definitions and views of social movements have been offered over the years.[2] Several notions are common to most of these and provide an important analytic framework that informs this study. First, social movements are fundamentally concerned with social change—specifically, with some redistribution of power, wealth, status, or a combination of these. Social movements are not individual crusades, but rather collective efforts on the part of large numbers of people. Further, social movements offer a set of ideas, an ideology, that articulates what is "wrong" with the status quo and offers guidance for bringing about desired social change. Thus, social movements are defined here as conscious collective efforts that aim at redistributing societal resources based on some alternative vision or ideology of what society ought to be.[3]

Four characteristics of a social movement just cited—origins, structure, process, and ideology—help us analyze whether feminism, or any other collective belief system, qualifies as a social movement under this definition. A social movement needs to be characterized by three primary attributes: (1) origins that show strong concern for social change and a redistribution of society's benefits; (2)structures and processes that give evidence of a collective, widely based support network; and (3) ideas and goals that reflect a definite political ideology.

ORIGINS OF THE WOMEN'S MOVEMENT

No social movement arises out of a state of tranquility and euphoria. Social movements, like sleeplessness, have their origins primarily in states of anxiety and stress.[4] The women's movement, when analyzed, seems to have similar origins. But what do we know about social movement origins from a scholarly perspective? Do the origins of the contemporary women's movement have similar characteristics?

First, social movements seem to arise from cultural settings that are structurally conducive to such forces. That is, social movements arise in situations and societies where collective action is possible, if not encouraged, and where, simultaneously, conditions creating dissatisfaction are also present (Smelser 1963). The United States in the late 1950s and early 1960s contained clear potential for the political arousal of women. Women were more educated than they had been at any point in the past, and more aware of national economic trends, thanks to the ubiquity of mass media, especially television. In addition, women's participation in the U.S. labor force was increasing at the same time that a decline was occurring in women's economic position and status within the labor force. Work opportunities were on the rise while the size of the average family was on the decline. Desires for a color television, a second car, better vacations, and college educations for children prompted countless numbers of U.S. women to return to work. The female labor force changed between 1940 and 1950 from one of predominantly single women under 25 to one of mothers and married women over 40. Yet those job opportunities in 1950 were even more sex-stratified than they had been in 1940. Jobs that were available were primarily the traditional female ones of secretary, nurse, teacher, social worker, and the like, while women's slice of better-paid, professional and technical jobs had dropped by approximately 30 percent.[5] Structural factors conducive to the emergence of the women's movement were indeed present.

But such structural factors alone are never adequate. The existence of such conditions is not enough. Widespread awareness of those conditions also is necessary. Thus, a second and somewhat more tangible determinant of social movements is structural strain, or cultural inconsistency— commonly expressed as discontent and unrest. Indeed, cultural inconsistency or outright contradiction was becoming more and more evident to women in the 1950s and 1960s. As Betty Friedan so aptly described in *The Feminine Mystique* (1963), the suburban dream of American housewifely happiness was souring rapidly. Concomitantly, the growing civil rights movement was reminding all Americans of the promises of equality embodied in even the traditional ideology. Yet even with a return to the labor force, greater political involvement in radical, new left, and civil rights efforts, lower fertility rates, higher education levels, and greater talk of equality, American women were awakening to find not the equal status with men to which they were beginning to realize they were entitled but, at best, a kind of quasi-egalitarianism that heightened women's influence in increasingly obsolete places. What women were discovering was the inconsistency of an egalitarian set of national ideals and a starkly inegalitarian reality. Put in terms of cultural conflict, the women's movement had at least a partial origin in the combination of increased idealism with regard to the concept of equality, a concomitant striving for personal self-fulfillment, and a rising awareness of the extent of the inequity confronting women. The product of all this was growing disillusionment and discontent.[6]

A third influence upon the women's movement soon followed: the spread of a generalized belief in the existence and prevalence of sexist ideology and practice. This belief spread unevenly and, at times, slowly, but it spread. Several tangible events marked its growth. Freeman (1975a) argues that President Kennedy's Commission on the Status of Women established in 1961 had a strong role in the growth of this belief. She argues that the commission's lengthy report, extensively documenting the unequal status of American women in society, left at least its few readers with the not surprising expectation that something significant would be done to alter this situation. Of far greater significance, I would argue, was the publication of Friedan's best seller, *The Feminine Mystique* (1963). With the reading, discussion, and media publicity given Friedan's book, recognition of "the problem that had no name"—housewife discontent—grew and became, at last, identifiable. The growing audience for this and other books[7] about women's place in society heightened the spread of a new, generalized belief about the consistently subordinate status of women, even if clear agreement was not reached about the cultural and historical causes or the appropriate solutions for this newly recognized dilemma. A clear and reawakened sense of the unequal, sex-based distribution of power and other societal resources arose in more and more sectors of U.S. society. Such an awareness became a focus for social unrest among American women and for their growing demands for related social and political change.

While the women's movement did not face a crisis such as a Watts riot, or a bombing of Cambodia, it did experience another quiet but far-reaching catalyst in 1966: the beginnings of organization. In the spring of that year a conference was held in Washington, D.C., for representatives of the state commissions on the status of women, the off-shoots of President Kennedy's national commission. Men and women came to this conference with the understandable hope that a governmental response to their studies would begin to remedy the existing unequal status between the sexes that was documented so clearly by the report of every state commission in attendance. But the conference participants left severely disappointed. Hence,

32 persons concluded that a strong national organization to fight for women's rights was essential if discrimination against women was to be combatted with even minimal effectiveness. Led by Wisconsin's Kathryn Clarenbach and New York's Betty Friedan, the National Organization for Women (NOW)) was founded on October 26, 1966.

Of less organizational, but far more emotional, impact, were two further incidents that seared the consciousness of many young college-educated women. In October 1964, Stokely Carmichael responded to a serious paper presented at a Student Nonviolent Coordinating Committee meeting entitled "The Position of Women in SNCC" with his now infamous remark, "The only position for women in SNCC is prone." Then, about a year later, Shulamith Firestone was verbally attacked at a Students for a Democratic Society meeting when she also tried to deliver a serious talk on the inequality facing women.[8] The result was a growing alienation of young college-educated women from radical leftist and civil rights politics, an alienation triggered not from these two incidents alone, but from a widely shared and growing recognition that these incidents reflected a pervasive sexism within male-dominated radical and leftist groups. The ironic product for women who had contributed personally to the fight for others' equality turned out to be the stark awareness of their own inequality.

Further causes of the women's movement were also to be found. Social, economic, political, and marital inequity and injustice were being blamed on specific social agents and institutions. Women were no longer accepting as their own the blame for existing conditions. As awareness of inequity spread, women increasingly focused their discontent upon specific targets—although not necessarily with any clear consensus. Growing numbers of women identified laws, gender and role stereotypes, specific men, and institutional and cultural patterns as the enemy. Some saw the enemy as more within—housed in women's own assumptions and behavior about what is appropriate and preferable. But despite the diversity of foci, root problems for women were being attributed to specific and growing numbers of social agents. Problems of women and their causes did not remain unidentified, diffuse, and, hence, unattackable.

However, no social movement succeeds without recognizing the effectiveness of organized action. Communication networks need to exist to persuade some large segment of the masses that collective (as contrasted to individual) action is necessary, and that value changes can and will result in less inequality and a new and better society.[9] The proliferation of consciousness-raising groups, the growth of NOW and other feminist organizations such as New York Radical Women, Redstockings, National Women's Political Caucus, Women's Equity Action League, and Female Liberation attested to the growth and strength of feminist communication networks.[10] Crucially, too, the failure of individual efforts of many women, multiplied and publicized a hundredfold, also contributed to the growing ground swell of recognition of the need for women to work together if they were not to fail separately.

Returning, then, to the criteria for defining a social movement, as set forth earlier in this chapter, we find that the origins of the contemporary women's movement satisfy the first two of the three criteria specified. First, origins of the women's movement centered in discontent with the existing distribution of social power, wealth and status. Such discontent was clearly one, if not *the*, principal cause of the movement. Feminists were and are interested in certain basic redistribution of social resources. Furthermore, the origins of the movement reflected a collective nature for the women's movement. Feminism had a broad base. It did not result from some individual, charismatic effort.[11] In addition, discussion of the movement's origins has hinted at, if not yet specifically set forth, the existence of a set of ideas—a feminist political ideology—that posits an explanation of the status quo and offers an alternative vision of the just society.

As has been true in numerous other mass responses to discontent, the *perception* of deprivation, oppression, and inequality seems to have been more instrumental in the generation and focus of discontent within the women's movement than was the absolute or actual position of the group (that is, women) within the society. Although women's position in the U.S. changed relatively little in the two decades after World War II, the perception women had of their status altered substantially. This growing consciousness, above all else, seems to have precipitated the current rise of feminism.[12]

STRUCTURE AND ORGANIZATION OF THE WOMEN'S MOVEMENT

Yet more evidence is available to suggest that the current growth of feminism represents the development of a social movement. Study of the structure and organization of the contemporary women's movement further buttresses the conclusions drawn from a study of feminism's recent origins.

Social movement theorists and analysts generally concur that although a movement aims at certain agree-upon changes in the social order, it does not necessarily have one overall formal organization in support of those aims. The organizational structure of a social movement can vary from extensive diffusion of power to extreme power concentration.[13] Similarly, no social movement can be expected to appeal equally to all segments of a society. If it did, a movement would reflect the dominant ideology, not pose a significant alternative to that ideology.

As pointed out in the discussion of women's movement origins, one key determinant in a movement's development is recognition of the need for concerted action of some sort. Proof in point of this recognition is the existence of movement organization. As Freeman (1975a, p. 4) has noted, "it is when the people most strongly affected by changes in social conditions are not already part of the policy-making process that they must organize themselves for political action."[14]

Some form of organization and structure is a necessary ingredient of social movements. Without them, we have spontaneous collective behavior, but not goal-directed movement. Any goal orientation is, by definition, an intrinsic part of the notion of social movements, for social movements are intended to reflect and embody social motion. They attempt to move groups from one point to another. Movements are not mere cathartic or therapeutic acts. They contain direction, and they possess some structure (or structures) for facilitating movement in the direction desired.

It has frequently been argued that the development of a modern, complex, technological society led to traditional groups' losing control over the loyalties and behavior of individuals.[15] As primary group loyalties are weakened, people easily experience a sense of alienation from the local community and the larger society. As associations weaken or a sense of frustration, coupled with powerlessness, occurs, individuals become ripe for new explanations of their dilemma, new paradigms to explain it, and new associations that provide hope of altering the reality in which they find themselves.[16] The structures and organizations of the current women's movement arose, at least in part, out of similar psychological processes. New associations were needed by and were born of women—in thousands of cities and communities around the nation.

Two structural arms of the movement, starkly different in terms of organization, but each vital and essential to the strength, growth, and effectiveness of the women's movement, were evident in the late 1960s and early 1970s. One arm, represented by the National Organization for Women (NOW), the National Women's Political Caucus (NWPC), and the Women's Equity Action League (WEAL), emphasized working through existing societal channels by accepted means and focused on reforming existing legal and institutional barriers to women's equality. The other arm expressed itself in the proliferation of consciousness-raising (C-R) groups aimed at overturning much of the existing system. Both arms arose out of discontent and recognition of the need for concerted action and mutual support, coupled with belief that change in existing values and behavior could occur.

As various observers of the women's movement have pointed out, organization of these two arms was markedly different.[17] The older, more reform-oriented branch of the movement established a clear hierarchical, national structure with elected officers, bureaucratic procedures, and jurisdiction of specific offices over particular tasks and issues. Consciousness-raising groups, on the other hand, prided themselves on their structurelessness, often taking great pains at revolving leadership tasks to maximize equality within a group. Such groups focused far more on personal growth and change, pursuing ideals of equal participation of members, internal democracy, and nonhierarchical egalitarian structures.

While blatantly different in organizational structure, the two movement branches shared a recognition of the need for concerted action, regardless of whether they saw the effects of such collective efforts as greater political clout or as a shared sense of sisterhood. Both branches recognized and tried to increase awareness of inequity on the part of supporters. Both promoted group consciousness, self-identification with the movement and with the plight of other women. Both were explicitly goal-directed.[18]

Increasingly in the 1970s, however, organizational similarity, if not a merger, occurred. Focus and emphasis tended more and more to center upon political efforts, upon tangible action that could affect change, and less upon consciousness-raising and support groups. The stress placed within the early years of the movement upon awareness and consciousness raising was more and more subsumed as a means to achieving social and political ends and less and less seen as an end unto itself. While consciousness-raising remains a personal goal for many individual women, explicit movement objectives increasingly treated consciousness-raising as an instrumental and not an ultimate goal.

Furthermore, the tactics of the two earlier branches have merged.[19] Groups previously considered more conservative—like NOW—currently espouse and actively lead in more radical efforts toward social change. The economic and travel boycott of states not yet having ratified the Equal Rights Amendment (ERA) is one such example. The coalition of the diverse groups of delegates at Houston for the International Women's Year Conference in November 1977 around the issues of lesbian rights and abortion opportunities provides another clear example. Lobbying efforts, both nationally and at the state level, have become both more intensive and more sophisticated. NOW has become an organization with over 100,000 members in all 50 states. At the July 1978 rally and march in Washington, D.C., NOW mobilized more than 100,000 persons from all over the United States to express support for extension of the ERA deadline. More and more, the National Organization for Women is recognized as the political arm of the movement, while other, differently focused groups, such as the younger National Lesbian Feminist Organization or the National Women's Political Caucus, pursue more specialized and individual goals. NOW cooperates with other feminist groups but has clearly emerged as that group looked to by most feminists for far-reaching political system change for women.

BUILDING MOVEMENT SUPPORT

Processes within the women's movement that enhance movement identification on the part of feminist supporters are directed more toward internal strengthening of the movement—that is, ideological and psychological movement support—than at external political goals (such as the winning of a court case or the passage of a piece of legislation). Understanding these processes further contributes to the conclusion that the present feminist movement is a social movement and not just some form of diffuse collective behavior.

As Ash (1972, pp. 11–24) stressed, social movements focus on ideological change for individuals and for society. Yet to focus upon ideological change alone without corresponding structural change is to doom a movement to failure. Ideological change is centrally concerned with "turning people's heads around," with helping them see the world in a new way. For a movement to succeed at fully or basically restructuring individual and social perceptions, however, a more radical level of social change and movement success is required: structural change within the society. The process is an interactive one. If radical change occurs within individuals but is never, or rarely, acted upon in society's institutions, far-reaching social structural change is essentially nonexistent. Personal ideological change must be combined with change on the systemic level. This is not an easy task. As Freeman (1975a, p. 6) presents it:

> Movements that conform themselves to the norms of behavior in order to participate successfully in political institutions often find themselves forsaking their major goals for social change. Long-range ideals are warped for the sake of short-range gains. But movements that hold steadfast to their radical goals and disdain political participation of any kind in an "evil" system often find themselves isolated in a splendid ideological purity which gains nothing for any one. They are paralyzed by their own fear of cooptation; and such paralysis is in turn the ultimate cooptation as inactive revolutionaries are a good deal more innocuous than active "reformists." Thus a successful movement must not only maintain a balance between personal and political change, but also a creative tension between its "politics" and its "vision."

The women's movement, like the black civil rights movement before it, politicizes the personal. Previously personal situations—for example, who cooks dinner or earns the family money, what kind of job one gets, where one is admitted to graduate school, what name is on a married woman's credit card, even the position one customarily assumes in the sex act—have come to be redefined by feminism as potentially, if not actually, political. The personal is the political. Personal change is a crucial social movement vehicle for more concrete political change. Organization alone is not enough. Attitude change by itself may not be enough. Political reform unaccompanied by attitude change is not enough. Attitude change that leads to personal behavior change on the part of hundreds or thousands is a more usual requirement for social and political change. Values and structures, both, require alteration if a movement is to succeed.[20]

Consciousness-raising groups, that arm of the movement directly focused upon value change, aim to put themselves out of existence. Their process focuses upon raising the level of consciousness, assertiveness, and confidence of members. As sensitivity of group members grows, increasing numbers of issues previously perceived as personal become recognized as political. Whether involvement in reform-oriented women's organizations results from membership in consciousness-raising groups or vice versa, both groups aim for continued sensitization to sex-role stereotyping and social inequalities related to sex.[21] Simultaneously, each offers support structures to members—recognition that their problems are shared and political, and are not just unique and personal. As Heberle (1951, chap. 1) stated about social movements generally, a sense of support and belonging are provided through movement participation. Unlike much of collective behavior, which may consist of a single incident, the women's movement, like other social movements before it, offers ongoing involvement in goal-directed activities with a common membership.

Contemporary society in its impersonality often discourages individuals from taking risks. The likelihood of effecting any desired change seems so slight in most cases that the costs involved for risk taking seem unjustified.[22] Through focus on specific agents as the parties responsible for social strain and discontent, a social movement provides a process that focuses risk taking on specific and appropriate targets. Social movements tell the discontented citizen who and what to blame. Movements increase the likelihood as well as the expectation that results will follow effort. Individuals come to see their concerns as shared, as commonly supported. Thus, action is encouraged—both by the movement's ideology and by other persons with whom the individual associates. Both the initial costs and the consequences of movement-related risk taking, then, are shared and, hence, lessened for the individual.

The processes of change involved in the women's movement are, theoretically, typical of those of other social movements. Consciousness of inequity and awareness of membership in the disadvantaged group result in attitude change on the part of movement followers. Such attitude change increases demands for specific reforms. Sensitivity to inequalities in tangible benefits of the social system—such as wages, for instance—often leads to recognition of power and status inequalities in other areas as well. The growth of awareness and of anger usually increases demands and group cohesion. As cohesion becomes more and more apparent to persons outside the movement, responses to movement demands usually also increase.[23] In this way, the social movement provides a vehicle for social as well as political change.

As Gusfield (1971, p. 446) described this process of change,

> The concept of a "social movement" is thus suggestive of people who, on the one hand, are in process of rejecting existing social values and arrangements while, on the other, they are both striving to make converts to their way of seeing things and dealing with the resistance that their activities inevitably call forth.

The focus of the women's movement, as Gusfield suggests above, is simultaneously upon profound value change and upon basic structural change. As we shall see in the discussion of feminism as ideology, radical feminists in their stress on consciousness-raising, and reform feminists in their concern with legal and relatively superficial structural change, agree that value change is essential—be it the aimed-for end result or a by-product. Unknowingly, they seem to share Talcott Parsons' assessment (1966, pp. 84–86) that changes in underlying value patterns bring about the most far-reaching social change. Thus, the process of change involved in the women's movement appears to be one in which personal change and political demands interact, a dialectic process integrating the personal and the political.

Essentially, then, the women's movement is a two-pronged effort that attempts both to change women's self-perceptions and attitudes so that each individual woman will be freer to pursue change and growth in her own life situation and, concomitantly, to alter institutional and structural conditions that inhibit women's efforts to gain equal rewards, recognition, and satisfaction. Feminists generally assume that the achievement of either of these two objectives will contribute to an achievement of the other, that each forges links in the process of social change. After all, if society treats and regards women as equal to men, must they not be equal? If women come to believe or, better yet, to know that they are in fact equal, is it not more likely that society will also treat them in a way consonant with their new self-perception?

The process by which feminism becomes established personally and supported within social and political arrangements appears to be one whereby: (1) inequities, injustices, and inadequacies in the treatment and position of women within society become personally and socially recognized; (2) women aware of and concerned about these conditions unite for support and political action; and (3) organized efforts are made to demand desired social change forcefully enough and for long enough that the system responds. This general process is inherent in social movements as a type and in the women's movement specifically. All evidence thus far points to contemporary feminism as a social movement. One last analysis must be made, however, before a conclusive statement to that effect may be made.[24] Does feminism have a political ideology?

NOTES

1. See, for instance, Etzioni (1972, 1966); Heberle (1951); Toch (1965); Freeman (1975a, 1975b); Smelser (1963); and Roberts and Kloss (1974).

2. Chief among these efforts are Von Stein (1964); Heberle (1951); McLaughlin (1969); Gusfield (1971); Davis (1930); Cantril (1941); Toch (1965); Ash (1972); and Roberts and Kloss (1974).

3. In the political science literature, social movements are usually included under either collective behavior or interest groups and political parties. Key referrents in the collective behavior literature include Smelser (1963); Kurt and Gladys Lang (1961); and Turner and Killian (1957). Under the rubric of interest groups and political parties, central sources would include Heberle (1951); King (1956); and Lowi (1971). Lang and Lang make a convincing argument for setting social movements apart from either categorization. Their chief contention is that social movements require both spontaneity and organization. Pressure groups and other voluntary associations lack the spontaneity of social movements, they claim, while mass collective behavior tends to be almost totally spontaneous and devoid of even the rudiments of organization.

4. One recent popular theory, however, posits the counter proposition that insomnia may actually result more from boredom than from stress.

5. Recent statistics, for example, indicate that the pay gap between men and women has actually widened rather than decreased over recent years. The March 1978 statistical report on the economic progress of women reported in the newsletter of the Project on the Status and Education of Women (published by the Association of American Colleges, 1818 R Street, NW, Washington, D.C., 20009) indicates that over the past 20 years economic conditions for women have actually worsened. Full-time women employees now earn 59¢ for every dollar earned by men *in comparable jobs*, compared with 64¢ twenty years ago.

6. See Juliet Mitchell (1971) on this thesis.

7. Such as de Beauvoir's classic *The Second Sex*, Eleanor Flexner's *A Century of Struggle*, Robert Smut's *Women and Work in America*, and the 1964 special and provocative issue of *Daedalus*, which focused upon the status of women in the United States and contained such controversial articles as Erik Erikson's "Inert Outer Space: Reflections on Woman-hood" and Alice Rossi's "Equality Between the Sexes: An Immodest Proposal."

8. See Seese (1969).

9. The extent of acceptance of such value changes is also indicated by results from various national surveys that show support for the women's movement to be greater than support for any of the other three "liberal movements" studies, approaching a majority base in most cases. The 1972 Virginia Slims Poll, conducted by Louis Harris and Associates, the 1974 Virginia Slims Poll, conducted by Roper, Inc., and the Institute of Life Insurance 1974 Poll reported in *Public Attitudes Toward the Family, Selected Findings from National Surveys* (New York: Research Services, 1974) are three such polls.

10. Jo Freeman (1975a, 1975b) has argued convincingly that a communications network was crucial in the growth of the women's movement.

11. This, of course, runs contrary to the self-delusions expressed upon various occasions by Betty Friedan. In fact, however, a very self-conscious—and, some would argue, politically restrictive—effort was made in the early years of the movement to avoid a "star" syndrome, to insure that leadership would be diversified and change frequently. This was especially true of the more radical groups, of primarily consciousness-raising (C-R) groups, in which rotating leadership was often required, and even within early NOW efforts and recommendations to newly organizing chapters.

12. Of course, the group "women," as contrasted to other social groups, is both larger and more diverse (and therefore more complex). With women falling within all economic categories, the amount and the nature of deprivation they received varied widely. Thus, no single "position" for women emerged except, as always, a position "below" that of men at comparable levels, whatever that level might be. Various U.S. Department of Labor data support such a contention, as well as a plethora of popular and scholarly literature document-ing or arguing the subordinate status of women in U.S. society. Of direct interest here is Gusfield's (1968) discussion of the relation between social movements and perceived relative deprivation (with Heberle as first author).

13. See Heberle (1951) for a summary of related early research on social movement organization.

14. Freeman (1975a) and Heberle (1951) are particularly helpful on this point.

15. Gusfield (1971) provides a useful application of mass society theory to the develop-ment of social movements. Gusfield sees highly industrialized societies as especially vulnerable to mass movements of various kinds precisely because of the growing sense of powerlessness on the part of so many individuals in such societies.

16. It is particularly ironic that in this "age of the individual," when so much stress is placed upon individual fulfillment and personal growth, so many individuals should be experiencing a marked sense of powerlessness in affecting the social structures and institutions that help determine the characteristics of their lives and the very values of individualism that contribute to their discontent.

17. Freeman (1975b); Whitehurst (1977, pp. 142–45); and Yates (1975, chap. 1).

18. For a discussion of the varieties of motivation for movement membership see Heberle's discussion of Max Weber's three motivational types in the International Encyclope-dia of the Social Sciences (Heberle and Gusfield 1968), "Social Movements."

19. See, especially, the extended discussion on tactics and strategy in the ideology section of this chapter.

Also note, Gloria Steinem's similar analysis of the growing unity of the women's move-ment in the July 1978 Ms., vol. 7, no. 1, pp. 65ff., in which she said that rather than the "conservatives" or "moderates" having taken over the women's movement from the "true feminist" few, precisely "the opposite is more the case—not because of a 'takeover' by 'the feminist few,' but because experience has made many of us more aware of the depth of the problem, and therefore more radical. The National Organization for Women, for instance, started out more interested in integrating a few women into the existing system than in transforming it for all women. Currently, however, NOW takes on most of the basic issues of economics and sexuality that it once shunned as 'too controversial.' In other words, it has become feminist—and accepted the fact that it is part of a revolution, not just a public relations movement.

"Relative to other movements and interest groups the Women's Movement is also measurably more radical. A 1976 Harvard University Center for International Affairs/Washing-ton Post survey of leadership groups in the U. S. (youth groups, the black movement, and many more) found that feminists were consistently more willing to address questions of basic change (public ownership of utilities and oil firms, redistribution of income, for instance) than any other group; and the majority questioned were members of NOW and the National Women's Political Caucus, the very groups often cited as 'conservative' feminists" (p. 92).

20. This, of course, is true insofar as social movements historically have defined their success in terms of the level of achievement of both goals: attitude and value change, and political change.

21. NOW often has C-R groups as part of the interest group structure provided in local chapters. Thus, membership in a C-R group and in NOW may occur simultaneously within the same unbrella organization.

22. See, for example, Cochran (1972, pp. 22–35) on risk taking and social change processes.

23. See Caplow's discussion (1975, pp. 202–3) on the role of perceptions of group cohesion as incentives for elite response to group demands.

24. Nordskog (1954) argues that the functions and goals of a social movement are determined by its ideology, its programs, and its goal statements.

3

FEMINISM AS
POLITICAL
IDEOLOGY

J ust as the question of whether the contemporary women's movement qualifies as a social movement has been the subject of debate, so also has controversy existed over whether or not feminism can be said to possess any set of ideas which can rightfully be called a political ideology. Freeman (1975a), Polk (1972), and Kontopoulos (1972) essentially concur that the women's movement began with no clear ideology and by the early 1970s, still had not developed one. Analysts such as Etzioni (1972), Chafetz (1974), and Yates (1975), on the other hand, argue that the movement does indeed possess such an ideology.

But just what is a political ideology?

Ideology in this work is defined as a political belief system that makes both cognitive (intellectual) and psychological sense out of political reality. The core part of this definition, of course, is that ideologies are political belief systems. This says, first, that ideologies are *systems* rather than disconnected beliefs. An ideology must be integrated and bounded. It also must be shared; expressed by some group rather than existing merely as a personal, idiosyncratic structure. Secondly, ideology is a *belief* system as differentiated from a set of attitudes, ideas or facts. Instead, ideologies integrate values and perceptions of facts into beliefs. Hence, an ideology is intrinsically "value" laden. Furthermore, an ideology is also a *political* belief system whose focus is upon political arenas and not primarily religious, aesthetic, or social life. Ideologies are complex phenomena. They are simultaneously intellectual and psychological, manifest and latent, empirical and normative. Ideologies are meaning systems, not simply knowledge sets.

They are interpretive and explanatory, providing the individual with a framework for finding meaning in the political realities of life.

If we are now to contend that the diverse views of the women's movement form a political ideology, these views must fulfill three requirements for ideological content. They must, first, describe present reality so that it is perceived in some new way. Secondly, they must explain that reality—that is, show how it has developed historically and in what ways that reality is good or bad. Thirdly, an ideology must posit a plan of action for changing present reality in pursuit of its stated values and goals. In other words, a political ideology must discuss what is, evaluate what ought to be, and suggest ways to bring that desired state into being. Ideology offers a new paradigm of experience. No social movement can be fully or properly understood without an understanding of the new or altered paradigm that it offers to society.

Scholar after scholar has reminded us that ideology is central to the success of a social movement. A system of generalized beliefs and commitment to those beliefs is what most clearly differentiates a social movement from other forms of collective behavior. According to Gusfield (1971, p. 446), social movements are "socially shared demands for change in some aspect of the social order." Social movements represent an explicit and conscious indictment of part or all of the existing structures, plus explicit demands for social, economic, or political change (or some combination of these).[1] Concern with liberty and equality is generally central to the demands put forth by social movements (Heberle 1968). As Barrington Moore, Jr. (1966) argues, widespread social agitation is reflected in social movements by a growing sense of moral indignation, a rising awareness of exploitation or victimization.[2] Perceived injustice can be a potent catalyst. It has been so for the women's movement.[3]

All generalizations require a focus on common properties, however. Feminist ideology is no exception to that rule; and, fortunately, feminism holds up a solid core of commonalities in its ideology to be examined. Although differences exist with regard to specific issues and the stands that different groups of feminist supporters take toward them, certain key elements of agreement remain with regard to the feminist description of reality, the values and goals of the women's movement, and the plans for social change found within feminist thought.

PERCEPTIONS OF SOCIAL REALITY

Consider, for instance, the descriptions of reality found within the women's movement. Feminists of different brands agree that sexism dominates U.S. society and culture and that the oppression of women is a prevalent pattern within that society.[4] Not all agree as to whether, or to what extent, exploitation exists, nor on precisely why female oppression has been so common historically in this and all other major cultures. However, clear agreement *does* exist that social, political, and economic discrimination between the sexes has been the norm rather than the exception and that certain common enemies of women exist within most if not all cultures—for example, marital structures and supports, economic and political power distribution, sex-role stereotypes, socialization patterns, and, in some cases, heterosexuality.

The Statement of Purpose of the National Organization for Women (NOW) illustrates this understanding of reality. Women are perceived as unjustly treated. Specific social targets are focused upon as the sources of this unjust treatment. Distinct agents of discrimination against women—education, government, business, industry, politics, the professions—are specified, and activism is advocated in combating this discrimination.[5] Feminism clearly assumes, and, hence, describes, a reality engineered by men. The existing male-oriented system is assumed. What is demanded here, however, is not a total questioning of the existing value structure, but inclusion of women within it. As NOW's founding document states,

> The purpose of NOW is to take action to bring women into full participation in the mainstream of American society now, exercising all the privileges and responsibilities thereof in *truly equal partnership with men*. . . . WE BELIEVE THAT women will do most to create a new image of women by acting now, and by speaking out in behalf of their own equality, freedom and human dignity—not in pleas for special privilege, nor in enmity toward men, who are also victims of the current half-equality between the sexes—but in active, self-respecting partnership with men. By so doing, women will develop confidence in their life, their choices, their future and their society. (italics added)

Rather than positing a major attack against the system, such early reform feminism asked for inclusion within the system. The focus was on "full and equal participation of women in the *existing* structures of society" (italics added).[6] Even these more conservative statments of feminism, however, described women as subjected to extreme discrimination. Building on the old feminist suffragette movement, which focused upon discrimination with regard to voting rights, the newer feminism described and criticized numerous additional forms of sex discrimination that existed in the 1960s (and, for that matter, in the mid and late 1970s for the most part as well). Women were seen as having been consistently subordinated to a secondary status that prevented or seriously inhibited their participation in the primary decision-making arenas of modern life—such as politics, industry, and philanthropic and institutional boards. Chief proponents of this view included such writers as Betty Friedan and Caroline Bird, and feminist organizations such as NOW, Women's Equity Action League (WEAL), and the National Women's Political Caucus.

Betty Friedan (1963), of course, described the contemporary woman's position in the early 1960s as defined largely by "the feminine mystique."[7] She described women as feeling lost, discouraged, unfulfilled, in spite of possessing all the external indicators of success of the customary American myth—prosperous husbands, healthy and happy children, well-kept suburban homes. In Friedan's analysis, "the problem that had no name" was the result of the acceptance by women, individually and collectively, of the traditional sexist assumption that men and women were intrinsically different from one another and, therefore, should and would receive their satisfactions from very different sources; at the same time, women found themselves disenchanted and unhappy. Friedan described women by the thousands who were dissatisfied with the substance and the trappings of "the female realm."

What women were beginning to be aware of, as she saw it, was the prevailing ideology of sexism. In a society where the dominant ideology demanded justice, equality, and freedom for all, the existence of widespread inequity and discrimination, if not oppression, had to be rationalized. That rationalization was presented in the form of sexist ideology that claimed that "natural" differences between the sexes required differences in treatment; these, in turn, led to the exclusion of women from primary access to sources of power, status, and social opportunities. The inequality or inferior treatment of women in the economic and political realms was not evaluated as unjust by society because women were supposedly dominant in their "rightful" sphere, the home. It was not that women received nothing, only that they had their special place. After all, men did not demand equality in women's sphere or see their exclusion from domesticity as unjust. Hence, why should women so view their exclusion from men's arena? It must just be another quirk of female nature.

The very lack of dissent from basic assumptions of the prevailing ideology testifies to the ubiquity and the effectiveness of that ideology (Dolbeare and Edelman 1977). Similarly, so widely and approvingly was sexism accepted by most Americans that it was obviously part and parcel of the dominant ideology. Thus, sexism spawned the feminine mystique, which, according to Friedan (1963, pp. 37–38),

> says that the highest value and the only commitment for women is the fulfillment of their femininity. It says that the great mistake of Western culture, through most of its history, has been the undervaluation of femininity. It says this femininity is so mysterious and intuitive and close to the creation and origin of life that man-made science may never be able to understand it. But however special and different, it is in no way inferior to

the nature of man; it may even in certain respects be superior. The mistake, says the mystique, the root of women's troubles in the past is that women envied men, women tried to be like men, instead of accepting their own nature, which can find fulfillment only in sexual passivity, male domination, and nurturing maternal. . . . Fulfillment as a woman had only one definition after 1949—the housewife-mother. As swiftly as in a dream, the image of the American woman as a changing, growing individual in a changing world was forgotten in the rush for the security of togetherness. Her limitless world shrunk to the cozy walls of home.

Sexist ideology assumed women were basically different from men: psychologically, physiologically, and, in some ways, intellectually.

Friedan argued forcefully for the extent to which sexist ideology had been sold to the American masses—of both sexes. What she then did in her description of social reality was contend that these differences were false and that the prevalence of the "the problem that had no name" testified to the fallaciousness of the mystique. If women were, indeed, psychologically and biologically programmed to find complete satisfaction and fulfillment in housekeeping and child care, then why were so many women expressing extreme discontent? Why were thousands of American women basically dissatisfied and unhappy?

The answer feminists posed was the existence of sexist ideology and women's recognition that the satisfaction and fulfillment they ought to be feeling, according to this ideology, was often simply not there. Women were asking if something was basically wrong with them, or, worse, believing that there was.[8] The status quo had joined the "is" with the "ought." The psychic tension that resulted was affecting burgeoning numbers of women. Analyses such as Friedan's were required to awaken American women to the appropriateness of questioning their own plight and recognizing that it was the expectations society held out to them and not their own inadequacies that caused the discontent.

Adding fuel to this fire, Caroline Bird (1968) documented the economic realities confronting women as well. She presented data that gave strong evidence of the consistently lower pay earned by women and the difficulty of access to high-level jobs or even to lower-level jobs if these were in what traditionally had been identified as male occupations. Women were aghast. They had been unaware that they were so persistently subjected to discrimination, that they were treated so much less well than men, that their economic opportunities were, in fact, so limited and prescribed. Kristen Amundsen (1971, p. 98) amplified this perception of reality:

To sum up, the U.S. corporate economy is run, managed, and/or controlled with very little aid or hindrance from the women of the country.

Women have little or no representation among either the governing business elites or the hierarchy in labor unions that have a chance to direct and shape this enormous economic enterprise. That women are important as consumers is obvious enough, but the "countervailing power" of the consumer can hardly be said to be more than a fond memory or a distant hope in this age of high-pressure advertising, oligopolies, and price fixing. Given the present impotence of women as a pressure group in the political arena, the power void confronting women in this additional important sphere of our national life is very serious indeed.

While probably no feminists (or very few) would disagree with this analysis, many, especially those who describe themselves as radical or socialist feminists, do not see this analysis of reality as sufficient, as going far enough. Socialist and radical feminists alike believe the existing situation to be substantially more bleak than do the reform feminists.

The world view of socialist feminists is a relatively clear and coherent one. The thrust of their argument is economic. Socialist feminists see the economic order as largely determining a society's political, social, and cultural structures. Hence, their concern is much less with the political inequities that reform feminism focuses upon (although they, too, recognize these) and more upon basic economic relationships.

Socialist feminists agree that women's traditional place in society has been secondary or subordinate. But the cause they find for this condition is economic and not grounded primarily in attitudes and traditional gender roles. Norms and expectations are seen to flow from economic roots, rather than vice versa. As Benston (1969, pp. 1–2) put it,

> In arguing that the roots of the secondary status of women are in fact economic, it can be shown that women as a group do indeed have a definite relation to the means of production and that this is different from that of men. The personal and psychological factors then follow from this special relation to production, and a change in the latter will be a necessary (but not sufficient) condition for changing the former. If this special relation of women to production is accepted, the analysis of the situation of women fits naturally into a class analysis of society.

The linkage between economic conditions women face and other forms of subordination is integrally tied to the nuclear family. This relationship is explicated (Benston 1969, p. 20) in the following way:

> As an economic unit, the nuclear family is a valuable stabilizing force in capitalist society. Since the production which is done in the home is paid for by the husband-father's earnings, his ability to withhold his labor from the market is much reduced. Even his flexibility in changing jobs is limited.

The woman, denied an active place in the market, has little control over the conditions that govern her life. Her economic dependence is reflected in emotional dependence, passivity, and other "typical" female personality traits.

Other feminists extend this economic analysis of society to consider women's role in reproduction and its subsequent effects upon women's social position. As Mitchell (1971) explains it, women's absence historically from essential areas of production is a direct result of her role in reproduction. Assumed physical weakness has not kept women from being more central in the production process, as these feminists see it; but the way men have used maternity as an excuse to maintain women in an economically noncompetitive and emotionally succorant role has achieved that end. Mitchell (1971, pp. 106–7), for instance, argues that,

It is rather women's role in reproduction which has become, in capitalist society at least, the spiritual "complement" of men's role in production. Bearing children, bringing them up, and maintaining the home—these form the core of women's natural vocation, in this ideology. . . . As long as reproduction remained a natural phenomenon, of course, women were effectively doomed to social exploitation. In any sense, they were not "masters" of a large part of their lives. They had no choice as to whether or how often they gave birth to children (apart from precarious methods of contraception or repeated dangerous abortions); their existence was essentially subject to biological processes outside their control.

The "social cult of maternity" Mitchell saw reenforced by actual powerlessness on the part of women in the economic and social spheres of society. Women, both structurally and psychologically, seemed to be programmed by society into a position of powerlessness and subordination.

Rowbotham (1973), too, analyzed woman's subject status as highly intractable. She saw women as too dependent upon happenings within their own bodies and not sufficiently autonomous and self-directed. Sexuality and economics became so interrelated, in Rowbotham's view, that together they guaranteed women a place "down under."[9]

The result of such analyses was the socialist feminist argument that women are not just oppressed, as reform feminists contended, but that they also are exploited and exploited badly—through both misuse of their labor at home, which is unpaid labor, and misuse of their labor in the marketplace through persistent underpayment.

Still other feminists agree with socialist and reform feminists that women are both oppressed and exploited, but see the source of these problems not in the absence of political and civil rights, not in the existence of an economically based class system of society buttressed by sexist attitudes and practices, but, rather, in biology and sexism. Radical feminists find core causes of women's oppression and exploitation in the physical weakness that accompanies childbearing and women's natural stature, and in the resulting dependence of women upon men for physical survival.[10]

Radical feminism sees women's subordinate social position as the most basic and fundamental of all oppressions. The physical subjection of women by men is the first form of oppression in history, they would argue. Women's oppression, as viewed by radical feminists, occurred prior to the institution of private property, not as a consequence of that institution. Thus, it is the biological that radical feminists see as having made possible the economic structures that maintain women's position. Economic factors clearly accentuate women's condition but they are not the most basic cause of it. Biology and sexism underly economics (Benston 1968).

As the Redstockings Manifesto (1970, pp. 109–10) forcefully asserts,

III. We identify the agents of our oppression as men. Male supremacy is the oldest, most basic form of domination. All other forms of exploitation and oppression (racism, capitalism, imperialism, etc.) are extensions of male supremacy: men dominate women, a few men dominate the rest. All power structures throughout history have been male-dominated and male-oriented.

The result as radical feminists observe it has been maintenance of women as an oppressed class.[11] Reality is almost totally oppressive to and of women, affecting every facet of their lives, when viewed through the eyes of a radical feminist. "We are exploited as sex objects, breeders, domestic servants and cheap labor. We are considered inferior beings, whose only purpose is to enhance men's lives." (Redstockings Manifesto 1970, p. 111). Or, as other feminists have put it, man has persistently defined woman not in terms of herself but in relation to him. Women are not generally regarded as autonomous beings, but as "the Other." Rather, man is seen as the subject, woman the object. Man is absolute, woman is relative to man (de Beauvoir 1970, Kreps 1973). In this view, women's oppression exists independently of other forms of oppression, with women's oppression being first and foremost. Without the success of the feminist revolution, equality between other oppressed peoples and their oppressors seems doomed to failure.

A strong case is put forth to explain why this social reality has developed historically. Living intimately with men (in this case, the oppressors), as the vast majority of women do and have done over the ages, women have been prevented from seeing their personal condition as a political condition. The woman has been deluded (or seduced) into believing that her relationship with a man is some ongoing changeable interaction between two unique personalities and that, therefore, it can be worked through on an individual basis and repeatedly improved upon. Thus, women have become blind to the class nature of their condition, blind to the realization that the personal is, indeed, the political.[12]

Based on biology and institutionalized by women as well as men, other factors strengthen the common illusion that women need men, that men are central to women's happiness and, perhaps, even to their survival. The norms of patriarchy, the nuclear family, and heterosexuality are key supports of women's oppressed position.[13] From birth to death, women have been socialized to the appropriateness of male domination and female subjugation. Consequently, women have come to confuse the order of reality with the order of necessity, not to mention propriety. Women have become subjected to "interior colonization," to use Millett's term (1970), where personality traits present in the rulers (that is, assertiveness, agressiveness, free expression of anger, and the like) tend to be inhibited in the subjects as a class. Control structures have become almost wholly internalized, so that what is socially structured, if not determined, appears to be part of the "natural order" of things.[14]

These perceptions of social reality differ on certain points. Within each, however, several common and unifying elements stand out. There is clear agreement that women are unjustly treated, that they are maintained in subordinate roles and positions, and that they are consistently removed from most vital decision-making opportunities of society. Furthermore, this discrimination against and exploitation and oppression of women are seen by feminists as rationally justified within society by a dominant sexist ideology. While there is not clear agreement on the original causes of sexism—practice and prejudice, the economic structure, or biology— agreement does exist that sexism dominates social functions and relations and that women are consistently and perversely treated as subordinates and inferiors.

VALUES AND GOALS OF FEMINISM

Such overall agreement among feminists on perceptions of social reality extends to values and goals of the women's movement as well. Succinctly, these may be summarized as an end to sexist practices and attitudes and full equality for women in all areas of life. Thus, the obvious goal is whatever basic and far-reaching social change is necessary to equalize the opportunities and social rewards available to each sex.

The vision and the hope of reform feminism is a society not basically unlike the existing one in overall structure, but substantially different from the present one in practice.[15] Stress is placed upon equality within the economic order, in secondary and higher education, in the existing family anf church structures, and in the current political order, as well as control over one's own body (reproductive rights and sexual preference).

While all feminists agree on these goals, some see them only as the baseline and not as the end point. For many feminists, more basic changes are required in the existing social order before true equality can be seen as a realistic hope. Socialist feminists, for instance, proclaim the need for a basic revamping of the economic system so that women's exploitation and oppression are no longer buttressed by the profit motive as well as by past economic practice and attitudes. Radical feminists, to take another example, stress the need for modifications of family structure and practice.

Given their view of reality, socialist feminists urge women to join in the socialist revolution (or evolution) to help bring about the equality that exists in nature but has never been effectively expressed with society. Women need to pursue equality in society as "peers" with men; they need to have and to expect equal dignity, respect, and work.[16] Specific socialist feminist goals include unrestricted access to positions and rewards of society, equality reflected in codified law, conversion of domestic work that is now private production into part of the public economy, public support of 24-hour child care, communal ownership of much production, equal work *by* men in the home as well as *with* men in the economic arena, and the elimination—not just the changing—of gender roles.[17] Socialist feminists pursue a goal involving more androgyny than the goal of most reform feminists.

Clearly, socialist feminism is based on certain assumptions different from those of reform feminism. Equality for socialists is not mere equality of opportunity, but, rather, equality of rewards. Socialist feminists do not ask only for fair inclusion within the existing system: they hope to change the system itself in very basic ways. Socialist feminists are less concerned with the individual good and personal self-interest. They are more concerned with the social good of all women and, eventually, all men as well. Socialist feminists do not want shifting and flexible gender roles; they want the elimination of such roles altogether. If liberation is to occur, as socialist feminists see it, far more is necessary than legal and political change. The larger socioeconomic system requires basic revamping.[18] In liberal or reform feminism, class oppression is lightened because it is shared. With socialist feminism, the objective is not a lightening of the burden of oppression, but its end.

Goals of radical feminists are akin to those of reform and socialist feminists but extend even farther. Radical feminists recognize that men and women are different in certain biological ways. Recognizing these differences, rather than ignoring their existence, radical feminists ask for certain types of differential treatment to help neutralize such differences as well as to help offset the effects of millennia of discrimination and exploitation of women that resulted from these differences.[19] No superiority or inferiority between the sexes is advocated by radical feminists. Rather, they hope for a society that enables women and men to be equal to one another without assuming the male sex will provide the basic ordering principle or referent.

Abolition of patriarchy, greater sexual freedom and more sexual options, encouragement of alternatives to the nuclear family, efforts that enhance androgyny, and the end of gender roles are demanded by many radical feminists. Like reform and socialist feminism, radical feminism assumes that full liberation will benefit men as well as women. Men, through their liberation, would find greater flexibility in the provider role, and greater participation in the father and homemaker roles. Male liberation is recognized by most feminists, but is not a goal for radical feminists, as it is, oftentimes, for socialist feminists. Rather, the liberation of men is simply an assumed by-product of the liberation of women. As radical feminists perceive reality,[20] however, only full focus on the liberation of women and actual achievement of that liberation can result in the liberation of other people.

Overall, however, values and goals of the women's movement show fairly widespread agreement. The eradication of sexism—in practice and in attitude—is probably the most basic goal.[21] Commitment to expanding options for women in all spheres of society is another shared aim, as is freedom from oppression and from gender-role stereotyping. In addition, all feminist groups agree that equal rights are essential; legal rights are seen as fundamental. The ending of employment and other economic discrimination is an agreed-upon must. Feminists, generally, want an increase in political power. They ask for legal protection of their reproductive rights and safeguards to insure that women control the use of their own bodies. Substantive and not simply symbolic equality between the sexes is the ultimate goal of all feminists—be they reform, socialist, or radical.

PRESCRIPTIONS FOR SOCIAL CHANGE

Feminist means to achieve equality are diverse but clear. Almost all organized feminist groups simultaneously pursue a dual-pronged strategy: (1) structural systemic change and (2) basic attitudinal and value change. The reform feminist plan for social change is complex and multifaceted and only somewhat less far-reaching than the social change pursued by socialist and radical feminists. Increasingly, strategical merger appears to be occurring among feminist groups.

Reform feminists advocate greater flexibility in gender roles, shared responsibility in the home, and equally shared power in the political and economic arenas. The foremost plank in the feminist agenda of NOW, at this writing, is passage of the Equal Rights Amendment (ERA). Other efforts include litigation on as many fronts as possible, the elimination of public school texts that reflect sex bias in roles or language (or, at least, a substantial decrease in the numbers of such texts), legislation that recognizes the right of women to control the use of their own bodies (that is, abortion, contraception, lesbian rights, and the like), promotion of adequate day-care centers, no-fault divorce, homemaker rights, credit insurance for married women who are unemployed, economic boycotts of products that reflect sexism and of states that have not yet ratified the ERA, and so forth.[22]

The list of demands from reformist groups keeps extending and the number of supporters increasing. At the same time that demands and numbers of supporters have proliferated, tactics for social change among these groups have expanded and altered. Economic boycotts, legal defense and offense, use of the electoral process, lobbying, efforts to attract favorable media coverage, attempts to rally members to political activism, as well as numerous and diverse confrontations to combat gender-role stereotyping, all contribute to the tactics used to implement feminist plans for social change among women's groups, such as NOW and WEAL, that were previously considered by other feminists to be somewhat conservative and not adequately aware of the need for basic, far-reaching social change.

Most of these tactics are aimed at changes in the legal and political structure, but full achievement of any substantial number of them could involve basic changes within the traditional system that would be far from conservative in their effects. Efforts at basic attitude and value change are similarly diverse. Press releases, media events (demonstrations, protests), publication of literature, appearances by movement leaders on television and at various group meetings, and the like all are aimed at attitude change. A clear interaction between attitudinal change and structural change is assumed by movement strategists—that is, feminists believe that if basic changes occur in the way structures relate to women, society will change the ways it thinks about women. Similarly, feminists believe that if enough members of society come to regard women differently, then the social structures that society sets up to maintain traditional values and distribute social benefits will also change.

Increasingly, feminists of all brands have come to see the ultimate necessity of both types of social change: widespread personal change in attitudes and behavior, and basic structural change within the system. Radical feminists now acknowledge, on the whole, that to change individual attitudes without changing structures is probably a futile and short-lived effort. Similarly, feminists primarily concerned with legal, economic, or political structural change generally acknowledge that to maintain and safeguard such change, widespread changes in individual attitudes and behavior are needed as well. Both fronts—attitudes and structures—must be attacked simultaneously.

Socialist feminists place their emphasis within the economic sphere. The way to achieve equality, as they see it, is to eliminate the private ownership of much of the means of production and, thus, eliminate the class basis of society. Equal distribution of both rewards and work is needed before necessary social change is accomplished.[23]

For radical feminists, the battle against sexism is more fundamental than the battle against capitalism or the battle for legal and political reform. Men, women's subjugation to their own bodies, patriarchy, the traditionally structured nuclear family, and, in some cases, heterosexuality are the primary enemies, not the economic structure or sex role stereotyping. Economic and political oppression are seen by radical feminists as more symptomatic than causal. Sex-based oppression is seen as the basic oppression from which all other forms of oppression affecting women emanate.

Some radical feminists are separatists, advocating the separation of women from men. Their argument is that only after women have learned full independence from men can they hope to rebuild their self-image, to know deeply that they can interact with men as equals on either superficial or deeply intimate levels. Separatism is seen as an oasis, an opportunity for women to recuperate, to "get their heads together," a temporary but vital interlude for personal strengthening.

In its most extreme form, of course, separatism is lesbian radicalism— lesbianism as both a political and a sexual statement. Lesbian feminists undoubtedly make the strongest and most radical statements for feminism, even though—due to the heterosexual bias of most contemporary women as well as men—they are undoubtedly not the most clearly heard or listened to. Lesbian feminists make the ultimate assertion of independence from the male-dominated value structures of contemporary society. In every area of their lives, including the sexual, they proclaim that women can function satisfactorily without men.

Lesbian feminists do not necessarily hate or even feel indifferent toward men. They may actually experience deep, sincere caring and even affection for men. Lesbian feminists also may not be declaring their lesbianism for all time. On the other hand, lesbian feminists may be making a strong political statement through their lesbianism. They may be saying that they experience a basic distrust of men generally, that it may be possible in isolated instances to develop a deep and trusting relationship with a man, but that the chances of that occurring are so small and the effort required to bring that to pass so great that the costs seem far to outweigh the probable benefits. Thus, allowing a male to be one's partner in the most intimate of relations, where trust is probably the most requisite, only subjects that relationship to undue strain. Lesbian feminists also often assert that if one does support and care for women, this should be apparent in one's intimate and physical relationships. Thus, lesbian feminists may see hypocrisy in the heterosexual relations of feminists who are consciously bisexual but still refuse to choose sexual relations with other women over sexual relations with men.[24] Thus, theoretically and practically, lesbian feminism is an affirmation and loving of women as well as a simultaneous rejection of men; concomitantly it is a political and a sexual statement.

For most separatists—be they lesbian or heterosexual—exclusion of men is both an expression of anger and a positive tactical step to redress a psychological imbalance between the sexes that is seen to be millennia old and to do away with the prevalent female self-perceptions of inferiority. Separatism focuses on an enhancing female autonomy, assertiveness, and self-esteem.

Stretegically, separatism leads radical feminists to place greater stress upon consciousness-raising than is true as a rule for socialist or reform feminists. Consciousness-raising becomes a training ground for more-broadly-based female participation in other arenas. Radical feminists first work at changing the image women have of themselves, believing this will enable women to then change political and economic reality. Other feminists tend first to focus on the political and economic system, believing changed images will result from a changed system.

Feminists agree, generally, however, that a strong self-image and widespread attitude change are crucial both for women and for the social change the women's movement pursues. Feminists concur that major social structural change—in the economy, in politics, and in social practices and expectations—are essential.[25] Although there are ideological differences regarding which type of change first needs to occur, feminists recognize that a change in reality is likely to change perceptions and that changes in perceptions will contribute to significant changes in reality. Lawsuits, legislation, economic boycotts, consciousness-raising, and media efforts are all embraced as viable and helpful tactics. A counteroffensive against the dominant sexist ideology, through public bombardment with feminist books, art, films, and the like, offers alternative images to a society lulled into somnolescent acceptance of sexist ideology. Self-concept development and assertiveness training facilitate the process of social change desired by the women's movement. Basic strategy for the movement revolves around unity through sisterhood. Women agree they need to work in concert, not simply through individual efforts, to combat the conditions women face. Basic agreement exists that changes must occur simultaneously in personal images—in women's psyches—and in social structures if lasting and deep societal change is to take place. Feminists recognize that their plight is shared, that the personal is political.[26]

There *is* a feminist political ideology. It is not a monolith, but, rather, emerges from a diversity of feminist lines of thought. Agreement exists among feminists' perceptions of contemporary reality, on basic values and goals, and on essential plans for social change. The purpose of this study is to observe the extent to which that feminist ideology: (1) is believed; (2) differs between men and women; (3) relates to broader political attitudes; and (4) is acted upon politically by supporters of the women's movement.

NOTES

1. See Freeman (1975a, chap. 1); and also Shils and Johnson (1968, pp. 68–70).

2. See especially Chapter 2. In addition to perceived injustice, of course, a social movement also requires the articulation of a new way, a new society, a changed order. Hence, the movement ideology must show that features of human existence that were at one point regarded as part of nature—and, hence, as outside the realm of human control—are now susceptible to human manipulation. See Caplow (1975, p. 200) for further discussion of this view.

3. Some have seen ideology that reflects perceptions of injustice as central to the gradual improvement of women's position over the years. See, for example, Goode (1963, p. 56), who contends that "the crucial crystallizing variable—i.e., the necessary but not sufficient cause of the betterment of the Western woman's position—was ideological: the gradual, logical, philosophical extension to women of originally Protestant notions about the rights and responsibilities of the *individual* undermined the traditional idea of 'woman's proper place.'"

4. The terms exploitation, oppression, and discrimination are often used interchangeably by the general public, although their meanings are relatively distinct. Exploitation generally, and as used here, refers to misuse or inappropriate use of an individual's labor, physical efforts, and talent by another individual. Discrimination is differential and usually inferior treatment on the basis of certain group characteristics—such as race, sex, or ethnic origin. Oppression, on the other hand, is persistent and systematic exclusion of persons from the opportunities and experiences available to others. For a rich and provocative discussion of oppression as a theoretical political concept and of its research implications, see Sapiro (1978b).

5. NOW is often described somewhat pejoratively by analysts, and a minority of other feminists, as the reform feminist branch or the conservative women's rights branch of the contemporary women's movement. Reform feminism, by this description, portrays reality within a women-are-equal-to-men model. Reality is supposed to be egalitarian in the ideal, but with the reference point for equality generally being the male or masculine norm that already exists. In the late 1960s, it appeared that reform feminism asserted women's equality in existing institutions and spheres without basically questioning the values that undergirded and maintained those institutions. Such an ideology was originally perceived as dominating the various most widely respected movement organizations, such as the National Organization for Women (NOW), Women's Equality Action League (WEAL), and the National Women's Political Caucus (NWPC). Even with such a conservative feminist orientation, however, the effects of "reform" feminism, if fully implemented, would be nothing short of radical. Clearly, today, such categorizations are, at best, outmoded, and more and more these formerly "conservative" feminist groups have come to be "radicalized" in terms of both ideological perceptions of reality and espoused tactics and strategy.

6. Yates (1975, p. 36), for example.

7. Friedan (1963). The reader is reminded here that Friedan's work was based on more

than a thousand interviews with women and, while not empirically rigorous, was clearly more substantive than any mere polemic.

8. As Karen Horney (1967, p. 8) described it as early as 1935, "there may appear within our culture certain fixed ideologies concerning the 'nature' of woman; . . . that woman is innately weak, emotional, enjoys dependence, is limited in capacity for independent work and autonomous thinking. . . . these ideologies function not only to reconcile women to their subordinate role by presenting it as an unalterable one, but also to plant the belief that it represents a fulfillment they crave, or an ideal for which it is commendable and desirable to strive."

9. Rowbotham (1973). Simone de Beauvoir (1970) is less explicit on this but, clearly, in her extensive and classic analysis of woman as "the Other" she implies much the same thing.

10. See Jaggar (1977, p. 12); Mitchell (1971, part 2), Firestone (1970).

11. See Firestone (1970, p. 6) for a discussion of this point and also Dunbar (1970, p. 481) for an extended class analysis of women's condition. "In competing among themselves for dominance over females (and thereby the offspring) and for land, a few males came to dominate the rest of the male population as well as the entire female population."

12. See the Redstockings Manifesto (1970) for a clear example of this.

13. See Firestone (1970), for example. Patriarchy is defined here as a state or form of social arrangement characterized by the supremacy of the father in domestic, legal, political, religious, and sexual functions, including the practice of maintaining power, status, and wealth of the family or group within the male lines.

14. See Murray Edelman's latest book on this, *Political Language: Words that Succeed and Policies that Fail* (1977). Edelman presents an alarming, convincing, and highly provocative elaboration of a similar thesis to America's poverty class.

15. See copies of the *NOW Times* through the 1970s for repeated support of this assertion.

16. See Rossi (1969, pp. 3-16); Benston (1969); and McAfee and Wood (1970, pp. 415-33).

17. See Carden (1974), especially Chapter 1, for an interesting discussion of this.

18. Nancy McWilliams expresses this in "Contemporary Feminism, Consciousness-Raising, and Changing Views of the Political," in Jaquette (1974, p. 160), when she says, "A political being has no exclusively personal problems. . . . These have roots in political ideology and practice and have important political consequences. Women have learned that their personal problems are not individual or inevitable BUT are generalized, systemic, socially caused and common and they are solving these problems through political action." (The latter part of that quotation, that feminists are solving their problems, would clearly not be agreed with by many feminists, but the former portion would be commonly accepted.)

19. See Elshtain (1975b and 1975a, pp. 452-77).

20. See, for instance, Morgan (1970, pp. 512-53) and in Tanner (1970), the manifesto "Southern Female Rights Union Program for Female Liberation" (pp. 112-15) and the paper "Women Unite for Revolution" (pp. 129-32).

21. Sexism is generally defined in the work of Amundsen (1971, 1977), Bird (1968), and others as a pattern of discrimination comparable to that of racism. That is, it is assumed that sexism is exceedingly complex as a system, that it is based on social, political, economic, and psychological structures and pressures that tend to inhibit both the opportunities and the rewards available to a group with certain biologically rooted characteristics—for example, femaleness.

22. For fuller discussion of specific plans for social change within NOW refer to the *NOW Times*. The evolution of women's demands as reflected through the NOW newsletter presents a fascinating picture of consistent radicalization of previously "moderate" women. The November 1977 National Women's Conference, sponsored by the International Women's Year (IWY) and held in Houston, Texas, gave clear expression to this trend. Here, traditional groups such as the League of Women Voters and YWCA dramatically rallied behind NOW and more

radical feminist groups when individual group members supported such controversial causes as abortion and lesbian rights in overwhelming numbers. See the January 1978 issue of the *NOW Times* and the February 1978 issue of *Ms.* (vol. 6, no. 8), especially Susan Dworkin's "Ellie Smeal Brings NOW Up-to-Date" (pp. 64–68).

23. In addition, socialist feminists urge women to recognize that theirs is not the only oppression, that racial, capitalist, and tribal oppressions exist as well and are as insidious as sex-based oppression. Women are, therefore, urged by socialist feminists to fight their own fight, but also to join with other oppressed peoples to whatever extent they can to aid them in their fight.

24. See Radicalesbians, "The Women-Identified Woman," in Babcox and Belkin (1971, pp. 287–93); Abbott and Love (1972); and Johnston (1973).

25. Not all feminists, of course, agree on major change in family structure or in sexual mores as goals essential to the women's movement, but reference to popular articles and to poll results shows that increasing numbers of American women do support such goals.

26. The Houston IWY National Women's Conference of 1977 gave a striking illustration of that when NOW delegates, League of Women Voters delegates, radical feminists, lesbians, heterosexual women, black and white feminists, old and young women all joined in supporting the 26-plank program for action adopted there.

4

FEMINIST IDEOLOGY: CENTRALITY AND CONSTRAINT

*D*isagreement over the extent to which the U.S. electorate structures its political beliefs has characterized political scholarship. Controversy over the viability of the notion that ideology constrains political attitudes and behavior is no less lively today (Wilker and Milbrath 1970; Bennett 1973; Marcus et al. 1974) than when the classic article by Converse on this subject first appeared (Converse 1964). The related controversy over whether feminism can properly be termed a political ideology revolves around similar questions.

The theoretical argument of the last chapter was that a clear core of feminist ideology does undergird differing emphases within movement writings. Stress on differences rather than commonalities within this literature misplaces the focus for social scientists concerned with relations that exist among ideology, attitudes, and behavior. Yet the assertion that feminism is a political ideology requires empirical testing. Fortunately, such an assertion also aids in constructing the hypotheses that frame such a testing.

The period from 1972 to 1976 provides a unique opportunity to study the nature, spread, and influence of feminist ideology among the U.S. electorate. The time period spans the years between congressional passage of the Equal Rights Amendment, rapid passage of the amendment by more than half the states, and heightening debate about and opposition to the amendment from the vigorous and vociferous right. Only phenomenal inattention to news reports, to the changing images of women in advertising, and to rising numbers of families recognizing (if not confronting) sex-role conflicts within their own lives could leave most members of the electorate in that period unaware that substantial changes in women's social position were occurring. But how is one to study feminism as an ideology?

THE STUDY

Several approaches to testing the ideological nature of feminism are apparent. Feminism has been coalescing over recent years into a clearly discernible ideology about which general public agreement exists, and several indicators of this ought to be evident. For one thing, a belief system ought to show an ideological structure. Requisite components of that structure will be outlined below. Secondly, if feminism is an ideology, a relationship indicating that feminism influences or predicts certain other ideas ought to exist between feminism and political attitudes. That is, feminism should exercise constraint upon related political attitudes. Furthermore, feminism ought to be related to political behavior in some ways; feminism should make a difference in how individuals relate to the political system. Let us expand upon each of these notions briefly.

Feminism, if it is indeed ideological in nature, ought to give evidence of this in the following structural ways. For one, the interrelationship between items of the feminist scale should strengthen with time. That is, if agreement or consensus about feminism is increasing, then the extent to which agreement exists among feminists ought also to be rising. To measure the tightness of the ideological structure—that is, the economy of thought the ideology gives evidence of—the number of factors into which the ideology breaks down may be analyzed, as well as the strength of the interrelationships between the items composing these factors. (Coefficients generated by factor analysis allow such a testing.) Secondly, if feminism is ideological, then some relationship ought to appear between feminism and related political issues. That is, a certain logical consistency should present itself so that the response to one feminist item predicts the response to other feminist items. As Converse found (1964), differences occur in the interrelationships (or intercorrelations) between ideological items depending upon the ability level of the individual studied; Stimson (1975) supported this finding. Higher-ability persons tend to have the most constrained or predictable thought (indicated by high correlation coefficients). In addition, however, feminism should also show—if it operates as Converse and Stimson imply an ideology should—a clear relationship to liberal-conservative ideology; that is, an individual's liberal-conservative score ought to be predictive of the individual's feminism.

A separate issue bears testing as well. If feminism is saying anything special to women as contrasted to men, then some clear empirical indicators should be evident to show that feminism differs between the sexes.

Some measures should indicate greater salience or centrality for women than for men when we investigate feminism. Such measures might be found in the extent of unidimensionality as contrasted to multidimensionality found among the feminist items, among the proportion of each sex who define themselves as feminist, or in the associations found between being feminist and other demographic variables. If, in addition to providing certain cognitive referrents, an ideology also makes sense out of sociopolitical experience in ways that speak to the psychological needs of individuals, then feminism ought to be associated with certain psychological phenomena among women in ways that do not hold for men. In short, if feminism is more relevant to women than to men in some ways, one might expect greater constraint as measured by unidimensionality among female feminists than among male feminists, differing demographic associations, and different psychological profiles. These relations will be explored in Chapter 5.

For feminist ideology to indicate that it has a potential role in political and social change, however, feminism also needs to show predictive power for political attitudes and, ultimately, political behavior. In short, feminism should make some difference among the electorate's relationship to the political system. Specifically, if we are to say that feminism is acting as an agent for political change among American women, feminism should propel women toward greater political interest and involvement. Chapter 6 lays out more fully some ways in which feminists differ from nonfeminists in such political attitudes as perceptions of government responsiveness, political trust, protest approval, system and institutional support, and political efficacy. Chapter 7 presents evidence of differences between feminists and nonfeminists in the nature and extent of their political behavior. Local and national participation, as well as conventional and unconventional participation, will be analyzed at this point. The final chapter will bring these analyses together and suggest what they bode for the political future.

To get to that point, however, we need first to establish empirically that feminism is a political ideology. That is the central analysis to be performed in this chapter.

Five key questions need to be addressed to assess whether feminism can be called a political ideology and, thus, used in the kinds of analyses called for in measuring the associations assessed in later chapters between feminism, political attitudes, and political behavior. (1) Do the items measured in the feminist index relate to feminist ideology in a cogent way theoretically? Do they tap a wide range of feminist measures as contrasted to tapping a few items dealing with narrow issues? (2) What generally has occurred to feminist agreement scores in the years between 1972 and 1976? Are more people agreeing with feminist positions and values or is this a passing fancy of little contemporary relevance to political life? (3) Does any single underlying concept exist that has clear predictive power for a respondent's scores on other feminist items? (4) Can feminism be predicted in any meaningful way by conventional liberal-conservative scores? Does any clear relationship appear between feminism and more conventionally defined political ideology? (5) Lastly, does empirical testing yield clear indications of constraint among the feminist items? That is, does feminism predict other political attitudes? If the answers to these questions are affirmative, then we can assume that feminism as a belief system *is* ideological in nature.

THE DATA

Primary data for the study are provided by the 1972 and 1976 CPS American National Election Studies, conducted by the Center for Political Studies of the University of Michigan.* These data provide both a large representative cross-sectional sample for each year and a three-wave panel study (1972–1974–1976). The 1972 study included 2,705 respondents interviewed both before and after the November 1972 election. Two questionnaire forms were used. Primary emphasis in this study will be on the subsample of 1,109 respondents who completed both the pre- and postelection versions of the "Form II" interview surveys.

The sample for the 1976 study was a combination of three overlapping samples, each derived from the initial 1972 study sample frame.[1] The unweighted N was 2,248. When weights were applied, this sample yielded an N of approximately 2,868. It is necessary to apply the weight variable to obtain a representative cross section of the U.S. voting population, who in 1976, were residing within the 48 contiguous United States. Of the 1976 N of 2,248, 1,005 were part of the cross-sectional sample (self-weighted 1); 1,243 nonpanel respondents were added to form a representative cross-sectional sample of adults 18 years of age and over. This base of 1,243 respondents provides the primary 1976 data cited in this study.[2]

MEASURING FEMINISM

A core of 11 items dealing with sex roles, women's issues, life values, and the women's liberation movement were asked both in 1972 and in 1976.

---

*The data utilized in this study were made available by the Inter-University Consortium for Political and Social Research. The data for the CPS 1972 and 1976 American National Election Study were originally collected by the Center for Political Studies of the Institute for Social Research, the University of Michigan, under a grant from the National Science Foundation. Neither the original collectors of the data nor the consortium bears any responsibility for the analyses or interpretations presented here.

These items spanned and tapped a variety of components of feminist ideology; they included perceptions of social reality, value statements, and prescriptions for social change. In full, the feminist items were as follows:

1. Women's role:
   Recently there has been a lot of talk about women's rights. Some people feel that women should have an equal role with men in running business, industry, and government. Others feel that women's place is in the home. Where would you place yourself on this scale, or haven't you thought much about this? (Scored on a 7-point scale, a 7 indicated agreement with "women should have an equal role with men.")

2. Influence of women:
   Some people think that certain groups have too much influence in American life and politics, while other people feel that certain groups don't have as much influence as they deserve. What's your opinion of the influence women have as a group? Do they have too much influence (coded "1"), too little (coded "5"), or just about the right amount of influence (coded "3")?

3. Abortion:
   Still on the subject of women's rights, there has been some discussion about abortion during recent years. Which one of the opinions on this page best agrees with your view?
   Abortion should never be permitted (coded "1").
   Abortion should be permitted only if the life and health of the woman is in danger (coded "2").
   Abortion should be permitted if, due to personal reasons, the woman would have difficulty in caring for the child (coded "3").
   Abortion should never be forbidden, since one should not require a woman to have a child she doesn't want (coded "4").

4. Laying off women first:
   Sometimes a company has to lay off part of its labor force. Some people think that the first workers to be laid off should be women whose husbands have jobs (coded "1"). Others think that male and female employees should be treated the same (coded "5"). Which of these opinions do you agree with?

5. Women can't get good jobs:
   Which of these two statements do you agree with? Many qualified women can't get good jobs; men with the same skills have much less trouble (coded "5"). Or: In general, men are more qualified than women for jobs that have great responsibility (coded "1").

6. Overcoming discrimination:
   Which of these two statements do you agree with? Women can best overcome discrimination by pursuing their individual career goals in as feminine a way as possible (coded "1"). Or: It is not enough for a woman to be successful

herself; women must work together to change laws and customs that are unfair to all women (coded "5").

7. Perception of sex discrimination:
   It's more natural for men to have the top responsible jobs in a country (coded "1"). Or: Sex discrimination keeps women from the top jobs (coded "5").

8. Handling discrimination:
   The best way to handle problems of discrimination is for each woman to make sure she gets the best training possible for what she wants to do (coded "1"). Or: Only if women organize and work together can anything really be done about discrimination (coded "5").

9. Role socialization:
   By nature women are happiest when they are making a home and caring for children (coded "1"). Or: Our society, not nature, teaches women to prefer homemaking to work outside the home (coded "5").

10. Men have drive:
    Men have more of the top jobs because they are born with more drive to be ambitious and successful than women (coded "1"). Or: Men have more of the top jobs because our society discriminates against women (coded "5").

11. Women's liberation movement:
    We'd like you to rate some groups in American society with what we call a feeling therometer. Ratings between 50 and 100 (actually 97) degrees mean that you feel favorably and warm toward the group; ratings between 0 and 50 degrees mean that you don't feel favorably toward the group and that you don't care too much for that group. If you don't feel particularly warm or cold toward a group you would rate them at 50 degrees. How warm would you say you feel toward the women's liberation movement?

To tap feminist political ideology properly, the 11 items needed to reflect the range of feminist beliefs described in the preceeding chapter. Specifically, the items needed to represent all three cognitive components of an ideology: perceptions of social reality, value statements, and tactics for social change. Feminist ideology, like any other ideology, needs to describe, explain, and prescribe.

Face validity of the items implied consonance with a feminist belief system and was corroborated by a panel of judges. Each item tapped some component of feminism referred to in Chapter 3. Perceptions of role socialization, of sex discrimination, and of the comparative influence of women in society are basic to the core belief structure of feminism, as outlined earlier. Values about the proper role women ought to have in society, how women should be dealt with in regard to employment termination, abortion policy, and the goodness of the women's liberation movement are all integral components of feminism. Recognition of the need for women to organize and work together on problems confronting them, as contrasted to women working individually, is a social change tactic that feminists see as essential.

Agreement was unanimous on the coding of all 11 items. Judges were clearly able to agree on what responses were most feminist. With regard to ideological or content dimension, as contrasted to content direction, agreement was also striking, but not unanimous. As Table 4.1 shows, seven of the items were unanimously classified. These items are marked with an asterisk. Three of the remaining items received two or three votes in a second category. Only the women's liberation feeling thermometer showed clear lack of consensus about item type. In this case, exactly two-thirds, or 16, of the 24 judges classified the item as a value statement, and one-third, or 8, of the judges classified it as a statement of social change. No item was evaluated as tapping all three ideological dimensions.

As assessed by panel members, then, the 11-item feminist index did tap all three dimensions of ideology required by Chapter 3. Given the difficulty feminist groups have historically had in agreeing upon tactics for social change, it is not surprising that in this 1972 list the smallest number of items are found in this category. Equally unsurprising is the larger number of items that appear in both the descriptive and the evaluative categories, areas in which greater agreement among feminists has been evident.

THE SPREAD OF FEMINISM, 1972–76

Ideological scope or breadth as well as face validity is clear on the feminist items. But how significant are these items individually and as a

TABLE 4.1: Feminist Items by Ideological Dimension

| | Ideological Dimension | | |
Item	Description	Value	Prescription
Women's role*		X	
Influence of women*	X		
Abortion		X	
Laying off women first*		X	
Women can't get good jobs*	X		
Overcoming discrimination*			X
Sex discrimination perceived	X		
Handling discrimination*			X
Role socialization	X		
Men have more drive*	X		
Women's liberation movement		X	(x)

*Indicates unanimous agreement on classification by judges.
Source: Compiled by the author.

combined index? Does a substantial portion of the American electorate agree with feminist positions? How has this agreement changed over time? Table 4.2 presents summary figures showing answers to several of these questions: (1) What proportion of Americans gave a feminist response to each item, in 1972 and in 1976? (2) What is the mean response for each item in those years? (3) What is the statistical significance of the change in those responses over time?

These data capture a striking picture of opinion change among the electorate. On all but 1 of the 11 items (the exception being the need for women to organize to handle discrimination), clear measurable change occurred in a feminist direction. Among a startling 8 of the 11 items, that change was significant at the .05 level.[3] On no item did public opinion become less feminist. Perceptions of women's appropriate role and of the extent to which discrimination exists have altered noticeably within this short four-year period (between 1972 and 1976). In addition, positive feeling towards the women's movement has changed markedly as well—from a mean negative feeling toward the movement in 1972 to a mean positive feeling in 1976. This change is not drastic, but it does indicate rising

TABLE 4.2: Change in Agreement Scores of U.S. Electorate to Feminist Items, 1972–76

Item	Percentage Agreeing with Feminist Response		Item Mean[a]	
	1972	1976	1972	1976
Women's roles	45	50	4.5	4.9 (7)[b]
Influence of women	23	33	3.5	3.6 (5)
Abortion	40	42	2.5	2.6 (4)
Laying off women first	52	57	3.1	3.6 (5)[b]
Women can't get good jobs	44	61	3.2	3.6 (5)[b]
Overcoming discrimination	33	50	2.7	3.2 (5)[b]
Sex discrimination perceived	27	45	2.4	3.0 (5)[b]
Handling discrimination	16	21	1.9	1.9 (5)
Role socialization	29	50	2.9	3.5 (5)[b]
Men have more drive	31	50	2.9	3.5 (5)[b]
Women's liberation movement			45.9	52.5 (97)[b]
Feminism total			72.2	78.4 (148)[b]

[a]Numbers in parentheses indicate the scale maximum for that item. All scale minimums were 1.

[b]Significant at the .05 level. The "feminism total" or "feminism index," as it is referred to elsewhere, is simply the sum of the scores of the 11 individual feminist items.

Note: For 1972, N = 2705; for 1976, N = 2403.

Source: Compiled by the author.

legitimacy for the women's movement and, perhaps, rising commitment on the part of women to feminist-advocated social change.

But do these items relate to each other in any measurable way? Do they go so far as to show characteristics of political ideology?

Philip Converse's statement (1964) of what characterizes an ideology has direct relevance here. He argued that an ideology possesses three distinct characteristics: abstract objects of centrality, wide scope, and constraint. The scope of the feminism items has already been addressed in a theoretical sense and will be further tested in Chapter 5. Centrality and constraint are examined here.

IDEOLOGICAL CENTRALITY: THE UNDERLYING DIMENSION

Converse and others have argued that an ideology revolves around some central underlying dimension, that some one concept or core set of ideas holds the ideology together or provides its basic foundation. In looking at liberal-conservative ideology, notions of social justice or civil liberties were found to be central. However, the application of some central or unifying dimension was found to occur only among persons with higher education and higher political information levels. The implicit argument put forth was that skills needed to relate an abstract concept (an ordering dimension) to specific political issues are developed by formal education and concrete information. Persons with developed liberal-conservative ideologies tended to have high educational levels, to know a good deal about politics, and to use their liberal-conservative ideology as a cue in deciding what political party and what candidates to vote for.

Previous evidence (Sapiro 1976) indicates the concept of role equality for women may offer an abstract ordering dimension for feminism similar to that provided by the liberal-conservative concept (see Converse 1964; Stimson 1975; Marcus et al. 1974; Weisberg and Rusk 1970). Respondents in both 1972 and 1976 were asked to position themselves on the seven-point women's role scale presented earlier.[4]

Investigation of the women's role scale yielded several interesting findings. First, support among the national electorate for equal roles shot up markedly between 1972 and 1976, as indicated in Table 4.2. Secondly, strong evidence was found that the concept of women's role does act as an ordering dimension in the sense implied by Converse.

Table 4.3 displays simple correlations between scores on women's role and other feminist items. These are partitioned by ability group and by sex. The ability group is determined by the individual's combined level of education and political information. Education is expected to indicate in at least a general way the respondent's ability to manipulate abstract concepts (although it is clearly recognized that this may be a gross idealization of the

TABLE 4.3: Relationship Between Women's Role and Scores on Ten Other Feminist Items, Stratified by Level of Cognitive Ability and by Sex, 1976

Cognitive Ability Group by Sex	Standardized Regression Coefficient of Women's Role x Other Feminist Variables	Significance Level	N
Men:	.439	.001	398
Low-ability men	.189	.11	73
Medium-ability men	.453	.001	191
High-ability men	.556	.001	134
Women:	.470	.001	583
Low-ability women	.337	.001	147
Medium-ability women	.492	.001	316
High-ability women	.574	.001	120

Source: Compiled by the author.

United States' educational system). Political information here reflects factual knowledge about the United States' political system based on answers given to five objective questions (for example, How many years in the term of a U.S. representative?). Cognitive ability is perceived of as the ability to intergrate "knowledge" into a larger framework that includes abstract concepts.

Obtained coefficients displayed in Table 4.3 show very uneven levels of correlation for the three ability strata. (A clear selection bias must be noted, in that far greater numbers of the low-ability group did not respond to measures of role than was true for the medium- and high-ability groups of each sex.) Two findings are striking, however. First, a consistent and marked increase in coefficients is noted for both sexes as ability group rises. That is, the predicted relationship between response to the women's role item and responses to all other feminist items rises sharply as ability level does. The association between logically related feminist items is not random, as Converse argued ideological associations were for the majority of the electorate. Rather, feminist items operate as Converse argued ideological thought would operate if structured about an abstract object of centrality, a central unifying concept. Belief in role equality between the sexes appears to offer just such a unifying concept for feminism.

Second, it is interesting to note, however, that only 21 percent of women, as opposed to 34 percent of the men, fall in the highest ability group. In addition, the mean ability level of men (8.5) is higher than that of women (8.1). Thus, in spite of lower cognitive ability level—or, more properly, lower cognitive *attainment* level—women show greater consistency or predictability of thought with reference to feminist items than do men. Women's logical association on the items tested is slightly higher than that of men's at every level, but significantly so among low-ability persons.

FEMINISM AND CONVENTIONAL POLITICAL IDEOLOGY

But how related to conventional political ideology of the liberal-conservative sort is feminism? If a strong relationship exists and if that relationship, too, is stronger among higher-ability persons, then additional support exists for the contention that feminism is an ideological construct. Table 4.4 presents striking evidence of just such support.

Again, two clear findings stand out. First, coefficients rise as ability rises, with both sexes. Only the lowest-ability group of each sex fails to associate its feminist ideology with its liberal-conservative ideology. The extent of association jumps dramatically from the low- to the medium-ability group for both sexes and then again from the medium- to the high-ability group for women. The liberal-conservative score of high-ability women shows almost twice the predictive power that is shown in the comparable relationship for men. High-ability feminists appear to integrate their conventional political ideology with their feminist thought far more than do men. (Note: There is no significant difference in the mean liberal-conservative

TABLE 4.4: Relationship of Liberal-Conservative Score to Feminism Score, Stratified by Ability Group and Sex, 1976

Cognitive Ability Group, by Sex	Standardized* Regression Coefficient	Significance Level	N
Men:			398
Low-ability men	.01	.91	73
Medium-ability men	−.18	.05	191
High-ability men	−.24	.01	134
Women:			583
Low-ability women	−.02	.79	147
Medium-ability women	−.19	.001	316
High-ability women	−.42	.001	120

*Negative regression coefficients reflect the direction of coding on the liberal-conservative scale where "1" indicated a very liberal response and "7" indicated a very conservative response. Thus, the negative coefficient represents a rise in feminist score as liberal-conservative score "falls" or moves toward the liberal position.

Source: Compiled by the author.

score for the two sexes: $\overline{X}$ for men = 7.87; $\overline{X}$ for women = 7.82. Nor is there a significant difference on the mean feminist score for the two sexes.) The difference noted is one of strength of relationship, and it is a strong difference.

Feminism is related to conventional political ideology, and it does operate as Converse's findings predict ideological thought would operate, with regard to both a central unifying concept and liberal-conservative ideology. But, certainly, for Converse, constraint is the most central idea in the empirical study of political ideology. His focus, of course, is upon constraints of logic. The focus of this study extends past that, to discuss constraints of a psychological and sociological nature as well (See Chapter 5). But first, what of logical constraint? Does any logical constraint appear to operate with regard to feminist thought? Is that constraint structurally evident?

FEMINISM AND CONSTRAINT

Controversy has been keen in political science over the value of Converse's notion of ideological constraint. Much of this controversy centers upon a matter of emphasis—emphasis upon whether it is the *structure* of belief systems or the rationality of certain attitudes and behaviors that is most important. In short, the constraint notion itself is not questioned as much as what that constraint implies—that is, does it imply structural constraint or rational constraint?

Some political analysts (Marcus et al. 1974; Weisberg and Rusk 1970) argue that voters use several dimensions, not just one, about which to structure their beliefs. Most importantly, such thinkers contend that multiple dimensions in belief structures give greater evidence of sophistication and cognitive complexity than does unidimensionality. Such an argument implies that complex, multidimensional belief structure is more conducive to rational choice and predictable consistency than is unidimensional structure.

Stimson (1975), on the other hand, argued forcefully that the concept of unidimensional constraint is more useful than the concept of ideological multidimensionality. He found, strikingly, that individuals with the most complex views of the political world also tend to develop the greatest constraint or parsimony in their belief structures. As he put it (p. 153), "those who are capable of articulating the most dimensions actually use the fewest." In short, he was arguing that those who are ideological in their thinking show the greatest evidence of economy of thought. They can order or organize more things.

The analysis of feminist ideology thus far has already established a relationship between "rationality" of feminist thought and ability level. Expected responses to related feminist items and to liberal-conservative scores became more predictable as the ability of the respondents rose. This association was striking both with regard to the centrality of the women's role item for the feminist index overall and for the strength of the association between feminism and liberal-conservative political ideology. The most predictable thought occurred in the highest-ability group for each sex.

Hence, two testable hypotheses appear with regard to the relationship between rationality and constraint. If Converse's and Stimson's position is accurate, then the feminist ideology of the highest-ability groups should be characterized by the most constrained or unidimensional structure—that is, the greatest parsimony or economy of thought. If the complexity or multidimensionality-of-thought approach is most accurate, then the feminist ideology of the highest-ability groups ought to be the most unidimensional.

Factor analysis is particularly helpful and appropriate at this point for studying the data. Factor analysis is a statistical method that reduces complex data arrays into a more readily comprehensible format. Given some set of correlation coefficients for some group of variables, factor analytic techniques rearrange the data to ascertain whether some smaller set of components or factors is central to and helps account for observed interrelations within the data.

The assumption, here, is that observed correlations are usually the product of some underlying regularity in the data. In other words, it is assumed that some particular observed variable is influenced or determined by various other variables, with some of those influences operating on other variables in the set and others occurring just to the one observed variable. When one factor or influence is common to several of the variables in the set, it is said to explain some correlation shared between or among those variables. Variance that several variables share with some explanatory variable is presumed to be the product of some common factor. Often, then, some small number of factors can explain most of the variance in some significantly larger set of data.

No particular assumption is needed about the basic or underlying structure of the variables. Factor analysis simply assesses what linear combination of variables would account for most of the variance in the data. The first factor, or principal component, as it is called, thus gives the best summary of how the data are interrelated. The second component explains variance not explained by the first and gives the next best explanation of the underlying structure of the data, and so forth.

Rationalists reject the structural constraint notion and imply instead that the higher ability levels will be marked by more, not fewer, ordering dimensions in belief systems. Converse and Stimson present a contrary view based on notions of economy of thought. They argue for fewer structural dimensions as ability increases. Feminism offers a clear opportunity to test these differing views. Table 4.5 and Figure 4.1 show strong support for Converse's constraint notion and no support for the multidimensional argument. The higher the ability level, the fewer factors in the belief structure. (The cut-off point was an arbitrary, but standard, eigenvalue of 3.0) The number of variables with great explanatory strength (coefficients greater than .60) in the first factor increased as ability level rose. Furthermore, the first factor explained more variance in each case when the ability level was higher.

Two further indicators support the constraint view of Converse when tested against feminist ideology. First, the average variance explained by each factor rose with ability level. In addition, the factor structure obtained was least stable for the low-ability group, most stable for the high-ability groups. These findings concur with Stimson's findings on liberal-conservative ideology.

The conclusion is clear. *Individuals with higher cognitive ability have more constrained feminist belief systems.* Furthermore, the feminist ideological constraint evidenced by women is greater than that shown by men in every indicator of Table 4.5. When applying feminist ideology, women have more constrained thought than do men. But for both sexes the indications of constraint are striking and consistent.

Figure 4.1 presents a different, visual image of these findings as a means of simplifying rather substantial correlation matrices. Factor analysis (varimax method and orthogonal rotation of principal components) summarizes the data by ability group. By confirming the presence of dimensions or factors, this analysis gives information about the kinds and centrality of items chosen for analysis. Because all respondents are subject to the same items and the same number of items, the factors found are not in this case an artifact of variations in item substance or number. Such variations can be a problem in certain uses of factor analysis. Sensitivity to varying numbers and types of items cannot occur when each partition of the sample is being tested for the same variables.

The results of factor analyses presented in Tables 4.4 and 4.5 are based on the intercorrelations of the 11 feminist items presented earlier (page 43). Partitions by sex and by ability group were made. Only factors whose eigenvalues exceeded 3.0 (a standard cut-off criterion more stringent than Stimson's 1.0) are presented.

As for the constraint debate, fewer dimensions or factors should be found at the high ability level—if Converse's hypotheses are correct—and more factors at the lower ability levels. Exactly this occurred. Converse's logic is upheld by these findings. For both women and men, the feminism of the higher-ability groups contains fewer factors; that of the lower-ability groups contains the greater number of factors.

TABLE 4.5: Factor Structure of Feminist Ideology as Evidence of Belief Constraint, Partitioned by Cognitive Ability Group and Sex, 1976

Cognitive Ability Group	Number of Factors	Variables that Load > .6 on First Factor	Factor Variance Explained by First Factor (percentage)	Mean Variance Explained by Each Factor (percentage)	Percentage of Total Explained by First Factor	Item Content Sensitivity
Men: (N = 398)						
Low-ability men	4	2	28	14.3	16.0	High
Medium-ability men	3	2	35	16.6	17.6	Moderate
High-ability men	3	3	40	25.7	20.7	Low
Women: (N = 583)						
Low-ability women	5	2	23	13.0	15.1	High
Medium-ability women	3	2	51	21.1	19.4	Moderate
High-ability women	2	4	54	28.8	28.7	Low

Source: Compiled by the author.

FIGURE 4.1: Variance Explained by Each Factor of Feminism in 1976, Stratified by Ability Level and Sex

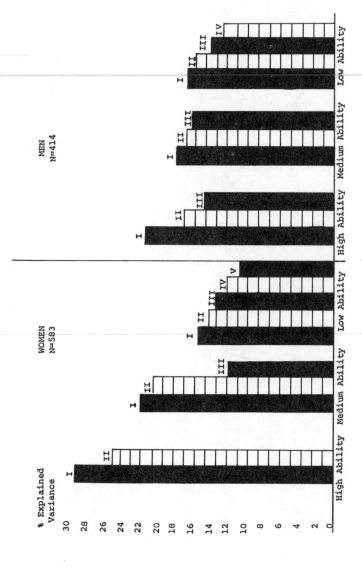

Source: Constructed by the author.

The visual presentation of what has occurred structurally in the feminist belief system of our population is clear. As we move upward by ability level on the feminist scale, the number of factors for each ability group decreases and the explanatory power of the factors increases. Fewer dimensions appear to encompass a greater nimber of concepts. Could it be that ideological thought does, indeed, become more complex, as the rationalists argue, but simultaneously more constrained structurally as well? That is, with fewer dimensions it appears that the sophistication of each single dimension increases. Economy of thought may allow more, rather than fewer, associations to be made for a single factor; that is, more ideas or attitudes appear to be related around fewer concepts. As Stimson implied (1975), could not less actually be more when it comes to ideological thought?

Figure 4.1 show clearly that the feminist belief structure for low-ability, not high-ability, persons is the multidimensional one. Weak explanatory power exists for each of the factors found among low-ability feminists, a finding substantiated by the regression analyses performed earlier in this chapter. The contrary, however, is true for high-ability groups, which are the most unidimensional and present the greatest constraint in their feminist thought. In addition, the explanatory power of the first factor for the high-ability groups is significantly greater than the power of the second factor—a finding not true for the lower-ability groups.

The findings are clear. Higher-ability feminists show greater economy of thought, more structural constraint, and more rational or logical constraint than do low-ability feminists. Furthermore, feminist women show even greater economy of thought than do feminist men. Rational and structural constraint are complementary rather than contradictory phenomena.

CONCLUSIONS

A picture has been outlined here of two conflicting notions about the structure of political belief systems. These notions have been tested on feminist belief structure. Attention has focused upon unidimensionality versus multidimensionality in belief structures of men and women of low, medium, and high cognitive ability.

After the theoretical scope of the items used here to measure feminist ideology was illustrated, a clear picture was drawn of increasing support for feminism among the U.S. electorate from 1972 to 1976. Given the striking increase that has occurred in such support, the belief structure of feminism was analyzed to determine whether it met Converse's criteria of centrality and constraint. Feminist scores on 10 items were found to be predicted by the score on the role-of-women item. The tightness of fit between this score and other feminist scores rose with ability level. The relationship between feminism and liberal-conservative ideology likewise rose as ability level rose. The relationship was strongest in each case for high-ability women.

Feminism showed itself to be structured around a central abstract unifying concept: women's role. Feminism was moderately to strongly predicted by liberal-conservative political ideology, with the strength this relationship, too, rising with ability level and greatest for women. Structural constraint was found in feminist belief structure. The higher the ability group, the fewer the number of factors for each sex.

Converse's approach to measuring ideology seems fundamentally sound. Strong support for his arguments is found with these analyses. Fewer factors and factors of greater explanatory power occur among higher-ability groups, all of which lends support to the notion that fewer factors, not more, are characteristic of greater rationality of thought.

Central to this study, of course, is the investigation of feminism. The overriding conclusion of this part of the study is clear: feminism appears to function as an ideological belief system. It gives clear evidence of centrality, rationality or predictability, and structural constraint. Empirically as well as theoretically, feminism appears to offer a new and increasingly accepted dimension of political ideology to the U.S. electorate.

NOTES

1. Further information about the sampling procedures can be found in Leslie Kish and Irene Hess, "The Survey Research Center's National Sample of Dwellings" (Ann Arbor, Michigan: Institute for Social Research, The University of Michigan), ISR #2315.

2. This was done by subsampling the 1972 sample of housing units at a two-thirds fraction (weighted, therefore, at 1.5). Ns, however, are in most cases smaller than 1,243, because only individuals who completed both the pre- and the postelection surveys were included. The reduced N for 1976 in most cases is 987.

3. On five of the items the level of significance was even greater: the .01 level. Those items were: laying off women first, overcoming discrimination, sex discrimination keeps women from good jobs, role socialization, men have more drive.

4. It should be noted that this scale appears to approximate more closely equal interval data than does a conventional Likert item and, in addition, is more abstract than Likert items, which generally ask respondents to indicate agreement or disagreement with specific statements. Both these characteristics are desirable for purposes of this study.

5

FEMINISM BETWEEN THE SEXES

*I*s there any reason to believe that contemporary feminism provides a catalyst that may alter the relationship of American women to the body politic? Answering that question is the central analytic task of this chapter.

Evidence was presented in Chapter 4 that indicates that feminism functions and is structured as a political ideology. Evidence of predictability or constraint among responses to feminist items was clear. A strong relationship was found between feminism in the high-ability group and conventionally liberal ideology. Yet, if the practical effects of feminism were the same for women as for men, contemporary feminism would offer little hope for propelling women into greater political involvement and activism than they have shown in the past. For any logical hope to be held out that feminism will significantly alter the role women now play in the political system, the associations and relationships found for feminism among women need to differ or give evidence of greater significance for women than for men. Otherwise, men and women would both be expected to change, but at comparable rates, which would be likely only to maintain the existing political imbalance between the sexes.

Few findings have been documented more repeatedly or over a broader span of political systems than the finding that women are less politically involved and less politically interested than are men. Data coming from at least seven countries and covering more than 20 years support such a conclusion.[1] While political differences between the sexes appear to be declining,[2] nowhere has women's interest and political involvement appeared to be fully equal to—much less greater than—that of men. If feminism contains the potential for affecting the role women assume within the political system, then it must do more than push men and women along in their historically unequal tracks. Rather, feminism must contribute to a measurable modification of women's previous relations to the political system. For if feminism simply maintains the already dominant political position of males in U.S. society, it will have failed in one of its major long-range goals: equalization of women's and men's position in the political power structure.

Several possible indicators exist that could show that feminism among American women is significantly different from feminism among men, that it might, indeed, help propel women into a relationship to the political system different from the relationship they have had in the past. These possible indicators tap a variety of measures: (1) extremism, (2) demographic distribution, (3) psychological linkages, (4) ideological structure, and (5) content.

To test whether feminism possesses the potential for influencing women politically in ways that it does not influence men, five sets of relationships were, therefore, investigated. First, a comparison was made of the distribution of feminism among women and among men. Two findings were expected: a higher mean in total feminist score for women and a greater proportion of women than men clustering in the tails of the feminism distribution. That is, women were expected to have a higher feminist score on the average than men and to be more likely to react very strongly either in support of or in opposition to feminism. Such a finding would be most likely to occur if feminist beliefs were more extreme, more intensely held, by women than by men.[3]

Second, the demographic correlates of feminism for each sex were compared. If feminism represents different things for men than for women, one would expect demographic differences to appear, especially with reference to certain life situations that are customarily associated with women. If feminism is not basically "different" for men, but is, perhaps, simply less salient or important for men than for women, such differences should not appear. The expectation was that the chief difference between feminism for men and feminism for women would be one of salience—that is, prominence, importance, or relevance to the individual. Thus, strong sex differences in the relationship between feminism and the demographic variables tested were not anticipated.

The crucial point in the argument that feminism has stronger explana-tory power for women than for men should be found in the relationship between feminism and key psychological variables. If feminism offers a way of seeing the world that differs strongly by sex, a key indicator of that should be the relationship of feminism to personal psychological constructs. A feminism that is salient for the individual ought to give evidence that it is more than cognitive, that it also taps important psychological dimensions for the individual. Salience of any attitude or set of attitudes is assumed here to reflect the centrality or importance of those attitudes for the individual.

Two other components of feminist ideology also provided important indicators of the comparability or dissimilarity of feminism between men and women and further indications of the greater salience feminism has for women than for men: the actual factor structure of the ideology and the content of the items that ranked most highly within that structure. Thus, the fourth focus of analysis was the factor structure of feminism and the fifth was the actual content of feminist items and their ranking for each sex.

SEX DIFFERENCES IN THE DISTRIBUTION OF FEMINISM

The first question to be addressed in any assessment of differences in the nature of feminism between the sexes concerns the distribution of feminist scores. Do more women than men support feminism? Is the mean for feminism different for men than for women? Is one sex more characterized by extreme scores on the feminist index and the other by more neutral scores? Or are no differences of this kind discernible?

A cursory glance at Table 5.1 indicates that the answer to the first question is no. Women are not, overall, more feminist than men. In neither 1972 nor 1976 does any significant difference appear in the mean of feminism for each sex. Thus, our first hypothesis with regard to feminism,

TABLE 5.1: Distribution of Feminism by Sex in 1972 and 1976

Feminism Score Category[a]	1972		1976	
	Women	Men	Women	Men
Antifeminist	20%	18%	18%	14%
Negative	37	34	27	28
Positive	32	36	42	46
Strongly feminist	11	12	14	11
Total	100%	100%	101%[b]	99%[b]
$\overline{X}$	74.7	74.0	78.2	78.7
	N = 629	N = 480	N = 590	N = 403

[a] Category or row divisions were made on the basis of quartiles of feminism score totals. The feminism score entered in all statistical computations in this study is simply the sum of the scores of the 11 feminist items described in Chapter 4.

[b] Sums do not always add to 100 percent, due to rounding error.

Source: Compiled by the author.

that the feminism mean would be higher for women than for men, is not supported. Women as a group are no more feminist than are men when total scores on the 11-item feminist index are used as the measure. For both sexes, however, an increase of roughly 4 to 5 percent is noted in the mean over the four-year period from 1972 to 1976. Both men and women are becoming more supportive of feminism over time, but neither is doing so at a pace that risks outstripping the other's.

The nature of the distribution of feminism by 1976, however, is striking. The proportions of women who are strongly opposed or strongly committed to feminism are, in both cases, obviously higher than the comparable group of extreme responses for men. That is, not only are women more strongly supportive of feminism, they are also more strongly opposed to it. The explanation that we would offer for this is salience.

Feminism is centrally concerned with *women's* role—a topic of interest, and in some cases, relevance, to men, but often a matter of self-identity for women. It is, therefore, to be expected that the salience of feminism for women would exceed the salience of feminism for men. What is interesting but peripheral to men may well be centrally important to women. The intensity of sentiment indicated by the extreme scores on the feminism index found in 1976 lends clear, if slight support to this explanation.

Favorable attitudes toward feminism generally increased between 1972 and 1976 for both sexes. Within this picture of generally rising support, however, lie some interesting sex differences in the distribution of feminism. For instance, the proportion of women scoring within either extreme range in 1976 equals 32 percent, as compared with only 25 percent for men. Only an unnoteworthy, and statistically insignificant, difference of 1 percent in the totals of extreme score responses existed for feminism in 1972 when women were compared with men. Thus, the change in the tails of the distribution over the four-year period presented is striking. In short, women were taking noticeably stronger, rather than more moderate, stands towards feminism in 1976 than was true for men. Judged by this finding alone, feminism appears to have a somewhat greater salience for women than for men. Support for this contention, however, at least as based on this finding alone, can be only tentative.

FEMINISM AND DEMOGRAPHIC VARIABLES

To the extent that feminism is principally a set of intellectual beliefs or perceptions of reality—that is, to the extent that feminism taps basically cognitive dimensions—demographic sex-related differences should be small. As feminism taps life situations peculiar to women, rather than a set of cognitive notions, sex differences should become more pronounced. The general assumption here is that feminism has a different relevance for women than it does for men. Such differences in the relevance of feminism for women, in the ways in which feminism says something about situations that fall peculiarly upon women, require that feminism be distributed differently between the sexes in terms of demographic profile. Thus, clear differences in the demographic profiles of men and women were expected only in those areas where feminism takes on a meaning or an emphasis for women that it does not for men. Overall, the expectation was that demographic profiles between the sexes would be basically similar. Table 5.2 presents some interesting, and unobvious, findings in this regard.

Socioeconomic Indicators

Socioeconomic indicators such as education, income, employment, and the like, and their relation to feminism, have changed noticeably over the four year period studied. The distribution of feminism for each sex, however, is amazingly similar with reference to these variables. No significant sex differences appear with respect to socioeconomic indicators and feminism. What is significant is the strong rise in the relationship between feminism and education. For both sexes; those with higher educational attainment are most disposed to espouse feminist ideas. Clearly, the overall educational level of the population has not changed measurably within this time. What appears to have changed is the level of acceptance of feminism, a change led by the better educated. What well may be occurring here is a beginning of the downward diffusion of values regarding appropriate sex roles, a value diffusion pattern common and well documented in many other areas (the spread and acceptance of divorce, the wearing of blue jeans as "chic" rather than functionally pragmatic, the food preference for steak among youths and adults of all socioeconomic classes, the equating of a ranch-style house with the American dream home, and so on).[4] What we have is a picture of growing support among the more educated for feminism. The pattern of the relationship between these socioeconomic indicators and feminism is one that, overall, is highly similar between the sexes.

Political Ideology As An Indicator

Given the above similarities between the sexes, is it not still true that feminism among males relates differently to traditional liberal-conservative ideology or party identification than is true for feminism among women? The answer again is no. Clear sex differences do not exist in these associations. Over time, however, these relationships show some interesting changes. First, there was no association at all among women between

TABLE 5.2: Regression of Demographic Variables upon Feminism Totals, 1972 and 1976, by Sex

	1972		1976	
	Women	*Men*	*Women*	*Men*
Socioeconomic indicators				
Income	.01	.06	.09[a]	.06
Education	.05	.06	.18[c]	.17[c]
Employment status	.02	-.04	.03	.09
Political ideology indicators				
Party identification	.00	-.10[a]	-.06	-.02
Liberal-conservative	-.20[c]	-.28[c]	-.14[c]	-.12[a]
Life-situation indicators				
Marital status	.08	.00	.18[c]	.07
Children	.04	.02	-.00	.01
Urban residence	.07	.04	.12[b]	.05
Age	-.11[b]	.06	-.17[c]	-.06
Race	.09[a]	-.01	-.03	.15[c]
Social integration indicators				
Union membership	-.03	.03	.13[c]	.07
Church attendance	-.10[a]	-.09[a]	-.12[b]	-.12[b]
Organizational memberships[d]	.08	.06		

[a]Significant at the .05 level.
[b]Significant at the .01 level.
[c]Significant at the .001 level.
[d]No comparable indicator exists for 1976.

Note: Entries are standardized regression coefficients.
Source: Compiled by the authors.

feminism and political party identification in 1972. By 1972 a slight relationship was evident. (The negative sign of the coefficient indicates a rise in feminism as respondents tend toward the Democratic affiliation responses.) Men have come to relate their Democratic Party affiliation less strongly with feminism in 1976 than they did in 1972, but the association is a weak one. Neither sex significantly associates political party identification with feminism in the more recent measure.

Such is not the case for liberal-conservative ideology, although, again, differences by sex are very weak. For both men and women, liberalism (indicated by the negative sign of the regression coefficients) is moderately related to feminism in 1972. That is, liberalism tends to predict feminism with some consistency. While this relationship is still significant in 1976, the most marked factor about it is its weakening over time for both sexes. Recent feminism is much less likely automatically to accompany a "liberal" political stance than was true in 1972. Rather, feminism is more evenly distributed now throughout the liberal-conservative spectrum than was the case in the early 1970s. That is, as the mean of feminism has risen over time for the entire population, so, too, has the diversity of its advocates. Party identification and political ideology are not significant predictors of feminism, nor are they significant predictors of differences in feminism between the sexes.

Race As An Indicator

Such is not the case, however, when we look at the relationship between feminism and race. Our expectation was that feminism would be more frequently espoused by minority women than by minority men. It seemed likely that, for minority women, feminism would be not only more salient but also different in certain respects from the feminism of minority men. The logic of this argument said that feminism for minority women might represent freedom and equality on several fronts—economic, political, marital—and thus serve as a general symbol of eased burdens and lessened oppression. On the other hand, it seemed likely that, for minority men, feminism might appear as a logical extension of basic civil rights but also practically imply the assumption of greater home-related responsibilities. Further, it seemed conceiveable that, as feminism was related to female job equality, for minority men it could also be perceived as a very real and imminent economic threat. Higher status for the one group still below minority men in the pecking order—women of any race—could conceivably threaten the minority male's status. Evidence in Table 5.1 and Table 5.3, however, does not support such an hypothesis.

In 1972, this thesis is given moderate support, as indicated by Table 5.3. Minority women strongly supported feminism in substantially higher proportions than did minority men. Far fewer minority women were antifemi-

TABLE 5.3: Distribution of Feminism among Minority Men and Women, 1972 and 1976
(percentage)

	1972		1976	
	Men	*Women*	*Men*	*Women*
Antifeminist	20	12	13	29
Negative	20	25	15	16
Positive	49	43	43	35
Strongly feminist	12	20	30	20
Total	100	100	101*	99*
	N = 41	N = 81	N = 40	N = 80

*Columns do not all sum to 100 percent, due to rounding error.
Source: Compiled by the author.

nist than minority men. But by 1976 a startling turnaround had occurred. Where previously minority men were antifeminist in almost twice the proportion that minority women were, by 1976 *the reverse is actually true.* Twenty-nine percent of minority women, as compared with only 13 percent of minority men, are strongly opposed to feminism. In fact, minority men show a marked reduction in their antifeminist feeling over this time. True, the die-hard 20 percent of minority women in the highest quartile of score totals remain constant, but the overall pattern among minority women is precisely the opposite of the one anticipated. Minority men have become more supportive of feminism than minority women. Why such clear disenchantment with feminism among minority women? Overall, minority women are still more strongly supportive of feminism than is true for white women, and by a significant margin (12 percent of white women versus 20 percent of black women in 1976), but the trend in support is reversed. For white women, rising support is apparent; for minority women, rising resistance is evident.

Item analysis of responses by sex and race discloses an interesting clarification of these findings. The only items on which black women became more opposed were: (1) support of the women's liberation movement, (2) belief that women need to organize and work together to overcome discrimination, and (3) abortion. Thus, minority women altered their opinions not on sexism or discrimination, but, rather, on how best to deal with these realities. Obviously, the "movement" is not perceived by minority women as the ideal way to deal with women's problems, nor is organizing together. Encouragement of abortion is also resisted—perhaps based on a fear of genocide or reports by minority women of involuntary abortions performed upon some of their members. The reversal of support for feminism or rise in resistance to feminism among minority women is related primarily to *tactics* and to the white-dominated organization that the women's liberation movement seems to represent, not to ideas of women's status or treatment.

A few observations are in order at this point concerning "the movement" itself. With the exception of Shirley Chisholm in 1972 and, peripherally, Barbara Jordan in 1976, no well-known black leaders come to mind as committed to or identified with the women's movement. In addition, the movement has been repeatedly accused of middle-class white bias—in membership and leadership, if not in objectives. Two examples of this are available. The first, a 1973 *Ms.* survey, indicated that the typical subscriber to that publication was white, college-educated (90 percent), and employed (75 percent). The second, a 1974 NOW survey, revealed that 63 percent of its members were college graduates and that a disproportionate number were also young and white. While sexism and sex discrimination may loom as very real facts of life for minority women, current tactics and movement efforts for overcoming these realities are not perceived as preferable or adequate. Part of this sentiment may well result from an inference on the part of minority women that the "women's liberation movement" as now structured is comprised of and aims first to help white women and that the needs of minority women appear secondary within movement efforts.

Life Situation Indicators

That sex differences in the relationship between feminism and race should exist was not altogether surprising. What was surprising was the reversal in those sex differences within the short time surveyed by these data. The explanation offered for these differences related again to salience—the centrality of movement tactics to the needs of minority women.

The meaning that an individual gives to events often differs profoundly with the individual's relationship to other persons and to the economic and political system that largely structures the opportunities available to all of us. The relationship of women and men to their life situation often differs markedly because of differences in the role (or roles) the individual plays within that life situation or in the autonomy the individual has to structure his or her life situation. Generally and historically, women have had less freedom and autonomy within the family structure than have men. Thus, in the relationship between feminism and variables that indicate the individual's life situation—such as marital status, having or not having children, age, and place of residence—one would expect sex differences to appear. As Table 5.2 shows, such sex differences exist.

Marital status, which was coded so a high score indicates an unmarried state,[5] is significantly associated with feminism among women, but not among men. While the relationship was stronger in both years for women than for men, the relationship became stronger for women in the period covered. Marital status does not bear significantly upon men's relationship to feminism in either year studied.

Interestingly, and unexpectedly, having or not having children did not relate to feminism for either sex. Urban residence, however, showed a relationship similar for each sex in terms of direction, but a much stronger relationship for women than for men. For both sexes, an urban residence associated positively with extent of feminist agreement.[6] The strength of this relationship was consistently greater for women than for men and became stronger by 1976 than it had been in 1972.

The relationship of age to feminism also shows women are affected differently by feminism than are men. While rising age was associated with a decline in feminism (represented by the negative sign of the coefficients), this relationship was far stronger for women than for men. The reasons seem fairly obvious. For young women, feminism is likely to signify not simply a set of beliefs, but a statement about life choices as well. Feminism may be an expression of change—not just change from parental values, but from parental life-style as well. For most men, feminism may involve an acceptance of greater job competition from women; but for many women feminism may involve a basic reorientation of how they direct their lives, a reorientation that is most likely to be evident among younger women who are exposed more extensively to new ideas and values.

Social Integration Indicators

Our last set of demographic variables, indicators of social integration, shows only minimal sex differences in relation to feminism. High incidence of church attendance is negatively associated with feminism for both sexes, a relationship that strengthens somewhat during the period in question. Organizational memberships generally show no sex differences as they relate to strength of feminism scores. But, strikingly, union membership does show a clear sex-rooted difference in its relationship to feminism. Women union members are clearly more likely to support feminist views than are union men; a finding not surprising in light of the threat that substantive economic equality for women could pose for the superior wage posture now enjoyed by many union men, nor in light of the acceptance of organized effort as an effective tactic to combat discrimination of various forms. Union membership, then, is the only one of our three social integration indicators that gives evidence of clear sex differences in its relationship to feminism.

The argument of this chapter, in brief, is that feminism for women differs in certain significant ways from feminism among men. Two sets of evidence have already been mustered in support of this view. First, feminism has been found to be both supported and opposed somewhat more strongly by women than was true for men—that is, scores on both tails of the feminist distribution were more extreme for women than for men. Second, differences in the relationship between feminism and certain key demographic variables were found to exist in relation to sex, indicating that feminism had a unique relationship with certain life situations that in some way impinged differently upon women than upon men. Marital status, urban residence, age, race, and union membership were the chief indicators of this phenomenon.

FEMINISM AND PSYCHOLOGICAL VARIABLES

We now turn to an investigation of the relationship between feminism and certain psychological variables to test whether feminism may be more salient for women than it is for men. The reasoning behind such a research question lies in the greater salience generally associated with emotional or psychological referrents as compared with cognitive or intellectual ones.[7] Extremism implied salience but did not offer a direct test of it.

Personal Trust

Feminism aims to sensitize women to their social and economic condition as well as to restructure that condition and remove inequities it contains. Part of such consciousness development is a recognition of oppression and discrimination.[8] Of the 11 feminist items, 2 focused on sex discrimination. Feminism attempts to heighten consciousness of the shared condition of women in other ways as well. On the one hand, the growing consciousness of discrimination and inequity within the traditionally male-dominated social structure clearly encourages greater distrust of that system and of those who appear to control power within it. We presume the latter trust relationship will be stronger than the first. One hypothesis we have flows from this argument: feminism among women should be associated with lower trust of people in general than is true for men.

In testing this hypothesis, an index of personal trust was formed by summing three items to form a composite score for each individual. High scores indicated a high level of trust. The three items included in the personal trust score were: (1) Can most people be trusted? (2) Do most people try to be helpful? (3) Do most people try to be fair?

Internal Control

Consciousness is often argued to be the defining element in individual personality. All that really says is that consciousness, our own unique sense of who we are and what the world is, is central to how we experience the self. Historically, women's self-concepts have to a great extent been dependent upon women's dependence upon men and the feminine attributes and roles that society run by men has imputed to and preferred for women.[9] One of the key indicators of this has been women's consistently lower perception of themselves as self-directed or internally controlled.[10]

In positing an alternative ideology for women, feminism attempts to mold stronger self-concepts among women.[11] One of the principal foci in such efforts is the sense of self-direction that individual women possess, here referred to as a sense of internal control. For this investigation, an index of internal control was developed that centers upon individuals' perceptions of whether life is largely determined by outside forces or whether they control their own lives most of the time. Four item scores were summed to give this index. Those items were:

1. Do you think it's better to plan your life a good way ahead, or would you say life is too much a matter of luck to plan ahead?

2. When you do make plans ahead, do you usually get to carry out things the way you expected, or do things usually come up to make you change your plans?

3. Have you usually felt pretty sure your life would work out the way you want it to, or have there been times when you haven't been sure about it?

4. Some people feel they can run their lives pretty much the way they want to; others feel the problems of life are sometimes too big for them. Which of these views most closely describes how you feel?

Two hypotheses are put forth regarding feminism and the sense of internal control women express. First, feminism will be more strongly related to a sense of internal control among women than among men. Why? A woman's self-identity seems more closely connected to role perceptions of assertiveness, passivity, and the like than does a man's self-identity. In short, it is argued that a relationship between feminism and sense of internal control is another measure of the salience of feminism for the individual. Second, the relationship between sense of internal control and feminism should become stronger over time for women but not for men. Such a finding would support the argument that the salience of feminism over time is increasing for women more than for men.

Fraternal Job Deprivation

Fraternal job deprivation, the only psychological variable not included in both election surveys, asked respondents, "How fair is what people in your line of work earn in comparison to how much people in other occupations earn?" Responses were scored on a range of 1 to 5, with a "5" representing belief that the individual got much less than she or he deserved, and a "1" indicating a perception that she or he received more than was deserved.

Many of feminism's political efforts have focused on economic inequities faced by women in the job market. Consciousness-raising groups and much feminist writing focus, among other things, upon greater awareness of the obstacles women must face in successfully competing in the contemporary U.S. economic scene. Of the 11 items in the feminist index, 4 related to jobs and perceptions of women's treatment in job procurement, advancement, retention, or pay. Our expectation is that women will have a greater sense of job deprivation than will men.

Life Satisfaction

Overall, feminism attempts to help women develop the personal tools and take the political and personal action necessary to increase their satisfaction with themselves and their own lives. Consequently, we wanted to investigate the relationship between feminism and life satisfaction. Our hypothesis is that feminism will be strongest among women with relative dissatisfaction with their own lives. Such dissatisfaction clearly enhances the salience as well as the relevance of feminism.[12] There appears to be no obvious reason why life satisfaction should be particularly associated with feminism among men.

These four sets of psychological variables—personal trust, sense of internal control, job deprivation, and life satisfaction—were chosen for testing because of their direct relationship to feminist ideology. With comparable measures available for three of these variables at both times, changes over time, as well as sex differences, could be noted. Multivariate regression was performed with the psychological variables as dependent variables and the 11-item feminism score as an independent variable. All regression equations (here and elsewhere in the analyses) were written so that age, education, income, race, marital status, and number of children were read in as independent variables before the entering of feminism in the equation. In this way, coefficients would not reflect spurious effects of these demographic variables. The effect of feminism upon the psychological variable measured is, thus, not contaminated by effects of these particular demographic variables.

Findings on Psychological Variables

Some important findings are reported in Table 5.4. Initial perusal of the table shows that psychological variables were significantly associated with feminism among women but not among men. Feminism for men simply does not tap the psychological dimensions that it does for women.

TABLE 5.4: Regression of Psychological Variables with Feminism, by Sex, 1972 and 1976, Controlled for Age, Income, Education, Race, and Marital Status

Variable	1972		1976		t_2-t_1	
	Women	Men	Women	Men	Women	Men
Trust in people	−.07	−.02	−.01	.04	.06	.06
Job deprivation			.12[b]	−.01		
Internal control	−.13[b]	−.05	.08[a]	.00	.21	.05
Life satisfaction	−.24[c]	.11[a]	−12[b]	.02	.12	−.09
	N = 629	N = 480	N = 583	N = 401		

[a]Significant at the .05 level.
[b]Significant at the .01 level.
[c]Significant at the .001 level.
Note: Entries are standardized regression coefficients.
Source: Compiled by the author.

Specifically, women feminists in both 1972 and 1976 tended to be more distrustful of people than were their male counterparts. While slight, these differences are consistent and support the hypothesis posited above with regard to trust of people among feminists.

Job deprivation is significantly associated with feminism among women, but not among men. The positive sign of the coefficient reflects a coding of this variable where scores rose as sense of job deprivation rose. Thus, the positive coefficient for women indicates rising feminism associated with a rise in sense of job deprivation.

Feminism's association with sense of internal control is, upon initial survey, strongly supportive of the first hypothesis posited concerning this variable—that is, that feminism will be more strongly related to the sense of internal control among women than among men. This is true in both 1972 and 1976. What is interesting about this relationship, however, is not only that it is a far stronger relationship for women than for men, but that the direction of the relationship changes over time for women. A startling change of .21 is noted. What the data appear to be telling us is that feminist women in 1972 were most likely to be aware of dissatisfactions, frustrated with their ability to control and direct their own lives. By 1976, however, for reasons not accounted for by our our hypotheses, feminist women seem to have acquired a positive sense of internal control. Is feminism reaching its goal of increasing self-directedness among women?

To state this a different way, the data imply that, in 1972, the higher a women's feminism, the more she was inclined to sense external controls dominating her life, a not illogical result of consciousness-raising. Perhaps a "need" (or, at least, a desire) for feminism is reflected here, a hope that control may be restructured so that reins are personally held. For men, only a slight association with internal control is noted in 1972, and *no* association in 1976. It is important to note here that these data do not indicate that women are lower or higher in sense of internal control than are men, simply that men's sense of control is not related to their feminism. For men, their sense of control is a thing apart from feminism. For women, it is closely connected, an important finding.

Again, in regard to life satisfaction, our hypothesis is strongly supported. We argued that low life satisfaction should be more characteristic of feminism among women than among men. Indeed, such is the case. While the relation between life satisfaction and feminism for men is positive in 1972 (that is, a rise in life satisfaction is associated with a rise in support of feminism), the relationship for women is just the opposite. The more dissatisfied with life a woman is, the more likely she is to score high on feminism. By 1976, the relationship between life satisfaction and feminism is weaker for women than it was four years earlier, but it is still markedly stronger than the same relationship among men. Feminism among men is not related to their satisfaction with life. Feminism is so related for women.

Two findings concerning the relationship between psychological variables and feminism stand out. First, feminism is clearly connected to psychological variables for women, but not for men. Second, the most far-reaching psychological constructs measured here—sense of internal control and life satisfaction—show the strongest consistent association with feminism among women and the greatest change over time. No such findings hold for men.

In addition to these sex differences in the distribution of feminism, the demographic correlates of feminism, and its psychological linkages, two possible areas of significant differences in feminism between men and women remain: differences in the ideological structure of feminism and differences in the content of feminism between the sexes.

DIFFERENCES IN IDEOLOGICAL STRUCTURE OF FEMINISM

The structure of feminist ideology was found in Chapter 4 to be characterized by two distinct phenomena. For one, feminism was found to revolve or be centered around the notion persons had of what women's appropriate role was—that is, of whether women should be in the home or should participate equally with men in various spheres. In addition, feminism was found to be most constrained with reference to its association with liberal-conservative political ideology when it tended toward unidimensional as contrasted to multidimensional structure. We need to ask, therefore, if sex affects these two primary characteristics of feminist ideological structure in significant ways.

Centrality Of Women's Role

Ideas of what roles are appropriate for women in society proved to be the central unifying concepts around which feminism was structured. When ability groups of men were compared with corresponding groups of women (as was done in Table 4.3), the perception the individual had of women's role showed itself to be more central to feminist scores for women than for men in each of the three ability groups tested. When responses of women were analyzed as a whole, a similar finding presented itself. As Table 5.5 shows, both the coefficients and the ranking for the women's role item are higher in 1972 and 1976 among women than among men.

Not only does the woman's role item load higher for women each year, but the strength of the loadings and the variance explained by the item became greater over time.

While this evidence of the greater centrality of the women's role item for feminism for women is not surprising given the evidence found in Chapter 4, the former clearly confirms the latter. How the individual values the equality of women proved to be a more central and unifying concept for women's feminist ideology than for men's. Feminism seems to deal basically with what it means to be a woman with and how a woman ought to act within contemporary society—issues that at first glance, considered empirically, seem to be more central to women than to men.

Dimensionality In Feminist Ideological Structures

Sex differences in the structure of feminist ideology are clear from the last chapter. Evidence presented in Table 4.5 showed clear differences in the cognitive structure of feminist ideology when factor analyzed. The number of factors for women was lower than for men in two of the three ability groups tested. The factor variance explained by the first factor was higher for women than for men in two of the three groups. In addition, the

TABLE 5.5: Centrality of Women's Role in the Feminism of Each Sex, 1972 and 1976

| | Total Variance Reproduced by the Women's Role Item on Rotated Factor Matrix | | Ranking of Women's Role Item on First Factor | |
	Women	Men	Women	Men
1972	.58	.50	Third	Sixth
1976	.78	.63	First	Fifth

Note: 1972 N for women = 629; 1972 N for men = 480. 1976 N for women = 590; 1976 N for men = 403.

Source: Compiled by the author.

TABLE 5.6: Factor Structure of Feminism for Women and Men, 1972 and 1976*

	Number of Factors	Variables Loading .6 on First Factor	Percentage of Factor Variance Explained by First Factor	Percentage of Total Variance Explained by First Factor
1972 Men (N = 480)	3	4	41.2	21.1
1972 Women (N = 620)	3	3	39.0	21.2
1976 Men (N = 403)	2	5	62.5	33.0
1976 Women	1	10	100	52.4

*Principal components procedure, varimax method, orthogonal rotation.
Source: Compiled by the author.

mean variance explained by each factor was higher for women than for men in the two higher-ability groups.

Further evidence of the structural differences of feminism for women as compared to men is presented in Table 5.6. In 1972, the factor structure of feminist ideology for women was very similar to that for men. This is akin to the finding that the proportions of each sex who gave score extremes were also very similar in 1972. At that time, the feminism of men and women did not appear significantly different. Comparisons were more striking in 1972 than contrasts.

But by 1976 a far different picture is presented. For both sexes, as Table 5.6 shows, factor structure has become tighter, the number of dimensions smaller. For men, the number of factors has been reduced from three to two. Strikingly, for women, however, *all feminist items now covary as one factor*. Furthermore, coefficients for all but one feminist item exceed .6 for women (see Table 5.7), an uncommon occurrence in most political science research. As these findings illustrate, the interrelatedness of the 11 feminist items is quite high for both sexes, but especially so for women. An exceptionally tight ideological structure is documented by these findings.

But couldn't a critic respond that women are simply more muddle-headed in their thought patterns than men are, and that this is the reason that feminism among women is characterized by only one factor as compared with two among men? After all, sexist folk wisdom has been telling us that for centuries. Perhaps women really cannot or will not discriminate among varying dimensions of an ideology.

TABLE 5.7: First Factor Coefficients of Feminist Items for Men and Women, 1976

Item	Women	Men
Women's role	.784	.052
Abortion	.719	.586
Laying-off women first	.653	.466
Women can't get good jobs	.754	.163
Overcoming discrimination	.668	.710
Sex discrimination	.781	.775
Handling discrimination	.551	.670
Role socialization	.737	.764
Men have more drive	.769	.074
Influence of women	.759	.541
	N = 1300	N = 943

Source: Compiled by the author.

Precisely the opposite conclusion seems to be supported. Findings here confirm those of Stimson (1975), which indicated that the simpler ideological structures actually tend to be associated with the most complex thought.[13] The paradox is apparent. Unidimensionality and constraint may occur concomitantly, strange bedpartners though they seem. Constraint appears to increase rather than diminish the number and complexity of associations that can be made around a unified belief structure.

Thus, with regard to both the centrality and the dimensionality of feminism, women differ from men. Findings indicate clearly, that, in both instances, feminism among women is not the same as feminism among men.

SEX DIFFERENCES IN FEMINIST CONTENT

The data above provided documentation of sex differences in feminist ideology. They did not, however, offer explanation. This last source of comparison holds the possibility for just such an explanation. Does feminism actually mean different things to women from what it does to men?

A comparison of the content of feminist ideology for each sex based on the factor analyses already discussed sheds light on the reasons for structural differences in feminist ideology. If the type of content of feminist ideology each sex emphasized were different, then the basic understanding the individual had of what feminism meant would also differ. For instance, a feminism that was primarily descriptive and emphasized perceptions of truth and falseness would be expected to differ from a feminism in which beliefs of what is good or bad, desirable or undesirable, dominated. Values are beliefs of the latter type (Rokeach 1973: p. 7). Values contain preferences, an emotional stance, and a behavioral component. A value is a belief that evokes feeling and upon which an individual acts by preference (Allport 1964, p. 454). Values are far more active and personally engaging than are more simple statements dealing with the truth or falseness of certain things. A finding that content emphasis within feminism varied, not randomly, but on the basis of the sex of the respondents, would, indeed, tell us something important about the nature and meaning of feminism to each sex.

Table 5.8 presents just such evidence. Looking first at the right-hand column, one sees that in both 1972 and 1976, the highest-loading variables in the first factor were descriptive for men. They were items ranked by the panel of judges as descriptions of social reality. Essentially, each item indicated how men saw the placement or problems of contemporary women. These items did not express values; they were not heavily emotion-laden by nature.

For women, on the other hand, a clearly different phenomenon was occurring. In both years surveyed, one of the two highest-loading variables on the first factor was a value statement for women. In 1972, a value statement concerning abortion loaded more strongly than did all but one other feminist item; and the value statement represented by the women's role item was an extremely close third. By 1976, the encompassing women's role item, a value statement, loaded more strongly than did any of the other ten feminist items for women.

Value statements dominate feminist ideology among women; descriptive statements dominate for men. For women, feminist ideology not only

TABLE 5.8: The Content of Feminist Ideology for Women and Men as Indicated by Factor Analysis, 1972 and 1976

| | *Two Highest-loading Items on First Feminism Factor* | |
	Women	*Men*
1972	Descriptive (Overcoming discrimination)	Descriptive (Women can't get good jobs)
	Value (Abortion)	Descriptive (Sex discrimination)
1976	Value (Women's role)	Descriptive (Sex discrimination)
	Descriptive (Sex discrimination)	Descriptive (Men have more drive)

Source: Compiled by the author.

tells them how the system is working, but also addresses basic questions of how it *ought* to function and what they should do to change the present system. This important difference in the nature of feminism for women as contrasted to men should not be lost or underemphasized. Personal preferences and beliefs tend to be more emotion-laden and more action or behavior-oriented than is true for beliefs about truth and perception. Values represent preferences and not just ideas. They indicate in a vivid way that some belief has special importance for the individual. Thus, the conclusion to be drawn from these data is clear. The actual content of feminist ideology has a different meaning for women than for men, a meaning with emotional and behavioral significance.

Other, but less striking, content differences also appear. For men, in both 1972 and 1976, descriptive items dominated the composition of the first factor, both in numbers of items and in the strength of the loadings. Value statements formed a second and less tightly structured factor for men in both years. The two social change items were divided, one in the first factor and one in the second, for men in both years as well.

For women, such was not the case. In 1972, the structure of the first factor was approximately equally divided between descriptive and value statements, numerically, with value statements loading more strongly than descriptive ones. By 1976, the unidimensionality of feminist ideology for women mingled statements of value, description, and social change into one factor. In addition, in 1972 the social change items loaded weakly for men (loadings under .5), but dominated the second factor for women, explaining 17 percent of the total variance and 33 percent of the factor variance for women. By 1976, these items were integrated into the single factor for women, loading at a respectable .67 and .55.

Content analysis consistently and strongly documented differences in the meaning of feminist ideology depending upon the sex of the respondent. The composition of feminism seemed clearly to differ between men and women. For men, feminism is primarily a set of descriptive beliefs about the state of the female sex and only secondarily a set of value statements. For women, on the other hand, feminism is first a value statement and secondarily a description of reality. Furthermore, feminism by 1976 had become a unified cognitive belief set for women. It was, basically, "all of a piece," a puzzle that seemed to fit together for women in a way that was not true for men. What ought to be, what is and is not occurring, ways to get where women think they ought to be—all these formed a cognitive whole for the female sex. By 1976, value statements, descriptions of reality, and tactics for social change were all woven together in the fabric of women's feminist ideology. Simply put, feminism means something different to a woman from what it means to a man.

CONCLUSIONS

Feminism *is* different for women from how it is for men. Based on 11 items answered by each sex, evidence was clear that feminism was understood or translated differently by men and by women. Feminism appeared to be more peripheral to men, more central to women. Evidence from five areas of analysis supports this conclusion.

First, feminism was characterized by more extremism among women than among men. That is, women were more likely to be either very supportive or very opposed to feminism than were men. Although the mean for each sex was comparable, the distribution of scores for men tended to fall more in the center or moderate range and less at the tails of the feminism distribution than was true for women.

Secondly, the demographic distribution of feminism, while comparable overall for men and women, showed feminism to be affecting certain key variables differently among women. Age, race, marital status, urban residence, and union membership did or did not exercise significant relationships with feminism depending upon the sex of the respondent, with strong relationships existing only for women.

Crucially, too, feminism among women, but not among men, showed itself to be psychologically linked, especially to a strong sense of internal control and low life satisfaction. The former association becomes especially important when we look at the vital role played by sense of internal control in the overall causal model presented in Chapter 6. Feminism, therefore, through these psychological linkages and through the greater extremism of its scores among women, has shown itself to be a phenomenon of greater salience for women than for men.

Furthermore, feminism is constructed differently as an ideology among women than among men, both with regard to the centrality of the women's role item as a unifying concept around which the other feminist items group and with reference to its dimensicnality. Feminism among women coalesced into one factor by 1976. Feminism is a more tightly constructed ideology among women than among men.

Finally, and importantly, feminism proved to mean different things to each sex. Actual differences in the emphasis or weight given various items comprising the content of feminist ideology were clear. Feminism among women is a construct that emphasizes values; for men, it is an ideology that emphasizes descriptive statements. Feminism for men describes the way things are. For women, on the other hand, feminism evaluates how things are and came to be and advocates ways to change them. Feminism is closer to being a "gut" issue for women than for men.

Inferences from these findings are clear. Ideology has both cognitive and psychological components. The cognitive dimension of ideology was carefully analyzed in Chapter 3. The actual cognitive construction of feminism followed the same general patterns for men as for women when partitions on the basis of ability groupings were made. Although higher-ability groups had more constrained ideological structure than did lower-ability groups, this was true for both men and women. The *pattern* of ideological structure was comparable between the sexes.

With regard to more psychological dimensions of ideology, however, feminism differed clearly between the sexes. Measures of extremism, psychological linkages, demographic associations, and feminist content all showed the pattern of feminist ideology between the sexes to be marked by differences more than by similarities. Thus, one is left with the broader inference that, for men, feminism is primarily a cognitive construct, while, for women, feminist ideology appears to weave together both the cognitive and the psychological dimensions into a comparatively integrated whole which provides structure and meaning to women's lives.

In addition, however, feminism differs between the races as well. The most striking and the most unexpected demographic finding of this part of the study involved the changes over time found for feminism with regard to race. This finding must be neither forgotten nor underemphasized. While the population as a whole was becoming more feminist, feminism among minority women was reversing itself. Instead of becoming more feminist in the time studied, minority women became more strongly critical of aspects of feminism related to tactics, abortion reform, organizing, and the women's movement itself. Practically speaking, women of color appeared to be backpedaling in an area where four years earlier they had been at the forefront. While more supportive of equality, and more aware of discrimination than any other group surveyed, these women obviously were identifying themselves less with "the women's movement" than they had been in 1972, and less than any of the other groups surveyed, even minority men, were.

Feminism, it appears, neither means the same things nor functions the same way for all people. Differences in feminism between men and women are clear and were explored here in some depth. Differences between white and minority women are also substantial but have not been examined extensively so far. Remaining chapters do that. What has been extensively documented, however, is the finding that feminism is different for different groups of people. Sex and race are vital mediators of feminist ideology. Just what these differences portend for women and how women relate to the political system in which they find themselves is the task remaining for the next two chapters.

NOTES

1. See, for example, Bertelson (1974); Verba and Nie (1972); and Haavio-Maunila (1972), for studies dealing with differences between the sexes in political efficacy. Participation studies that included women as a comparative group are numerous. A limited list would include, in addition to those mentioned above, Almond and Verba (1963); Miller (1972); Dennis (1966); Welch (1977); Soule and McGrath (1974); Andersen (1975); and Pomper (1975).

2. For instance, Easton and Dennis (1969) clearly found sex differences too small to be of great consequence for the operation of the political system. Welch (1977) and Andersen (1975) showed similar findings. Other recent studies have shown sex differences to be reduced in most areas of political participation and with reference to political attitudes such as trust and efficacy as well. See, for instance, Jennings and Thomas (1976).

3. Is actually living out feminist beliefs more difficult than men initially anticipated? Or are men just beginning to realize the far-reaching and often radical implications of feminism?

4. For a discussion of the "downward diffusion of values," see Cooley (1966); Young and Willmott (1973); and Parkin (1972).

5. The coding of marital status was as follows: 1 = widowed, 2 = currently married, 3 = separated or divorced, 4 = never married. Missing data were coded into the item mean.

6. Negative coefficients in Table 5.4 reflect the coding of residence, in which a "1" indicated residence in one of the ten largest standard metropolitan statistical areas and each higher number up to "4" indicated a more rural residence.

7. See Paul Sniderman (1975), Chapter 2, for a discussion of this.

8. See, especially, the recent studies dealing with black militancy, such as Rotter (1966); Caplan and Paige (1968); Gurin et al. (1969); Forward and Williams (1970); Rosen and Stalling (1971); and Mankoff (1968).

Obviously, marital status is a nominal classification. This coding scheme was an arbitrary effort to indicate greater and lesser degrees of marital attachment. The validity of such a classification scheme is, of course, subject to debate.

9. See Aberbach and Walker (1973); Pomper (1975); Verba and Nie (1972); Verba, Nie, and Petrocik (1976); Gurin et al. (1979); Sanger and Alker (1973).

10. See, for instance, Bardwick and Douvan (1971); Cochran (1972); Gove and Tudor (1973); Simon (1967); Goffman (1961); Holter (1970); and Jennings and Thomas (1968).

11. For effects of active involvement in the women's movement upon sense of internal control, see Riger (1977).

12. It is recognized here that the use of definition of self-concept is fraught with danger. See Sniderman (1975, chap. 2) for an extensive discussion of these problems.

13. Stimson (1975).

6

FEMINISM AND POLITICAL ATTITUDES

*E*ffects of ideology upon political behavior are rarely direct. More usually, political attitudes are crucial in translating beliefs into action. Numerous studies have shown this to be the case. When we examine the literature on political attitudes, we find that there are really two basic types of political attitudes that mediate between ideology and behavior, thereby influencing the ways in which an ideology actually gets expressed in a person's actions.

The first kind of political attitudes that affect this relationship is of a very personal nature. These attitudes reflect the way the individual perceives she or he can and ought to relate to the political system. A person's sense of political efficacy and citizen duty, political interest, and approval of protest are examples of attitudes of this sort. The second kind of attitudes involves evaluations of the political system itself, rather than of the individual and how the individual ought to relate to that system. These attitudes include such things as whether the government can be trusted, how well parts of the political system function, whether the government is attentive or responsive to its citizens, and so on. The individual needs to have strong feelings either about herself or himself or about the political system, before acting differently toward that system.

The first kind of attitudes, how we feel about ourselves in relation to the political system, is strongly influenced by our notions of appropriate and inappropriate gender roles. Perceptions of what roles are appropriate and inappropriate have a crucial effect upon personality development and how people interact with their social environment. Most persons want to be socially accepted. Most of us imitate, at times, the behaviors of persons we identify with and admire. Our understandings of what behavior is socially approved are greatly influenced by our perceptions of how society rewards and punishes individuals who act in certain ways. This is as true for how we understand social acceptance of political role behavior as it is in the case of other role behavior. Subtle and pervasive expectations of what is and is not socially acceptable political role behavior for men and women, thus, become established.

Further substantiation for the key role played by attitudes of the first type upon social behavior is provided by much sex role research (Bardwick and Douvan 1971; Cochran 1972; Gove and Tudor 1973; Simon 1967; Goffman 1961; Holter 1970; and Jennings and Thomas 1968). As role theorists argue, role perceptions are the crucial key in the interaction between individual personality and social behavior. Desire for social acceptance as well as needs of personal identity motivate the individual to want to play roles in ways deemed appropriate by reference groups. Colloquially put, we all want those we like and identify with to find our behavior acceptable, likeable, and inoffensive, and, again, this is as true for political role performance and expectations as for other types of social acts.

Historically, women's political roles have differed clearly from those of men. Leadership by women has been neither common and expected nor obviously desired in the political arena. Participation by women has been consistently lower than that of men, although differences have increasingly been smaller in recent years (Duverger 1955; Bien and Boynton 1976; Brody and Sniderman 1975; Amundsen 1971, 1977; Jennings and Niemi 1971; Easton and Dennis 1969; Verba and Nie 1972; Greenstein 1961). Still, the record of political life in the United States provides *prima facie* evidence that an activist political leadership role for women has not been perceived or generally acted upon by the female electorate. In 1978, there is still no elected woman senator; there are only 19 women members of Congress and only 2 women governors. Men virtually monopolize the U.S. political decision-making arena—whether we look to the past or to the present.[1] Women's role in politics gives but another example of how gender stereotypes get translated into sex-role stereotypes, which are directly related both to self-concept and to behavior (Bardwick and Douvan 1971). Women persistently are taught not only to *feel* a certain way in reference to the political system (that is, passive, nurturant, dependent, and so on) but also, and perhaps more importantly, to *act* in that way.

Changes in political role expectations, which feminism clearly hopes to bring about, involve changes in political attitude. Such changes in political role expectations are undoubtedly complex. For feminism, however, such changes could be reflected in a strengthening sense of internal control, of political efficacy, of citizen duty, and so on.[2] Personal political attitudes must change before behavior is likely to change. Something new usually must be internalized, accepted psychologically, before behavior change results. Yet Chapter 5 presented evidence that psychological associations with feminist beliefs are strong among many women. Those data provided a fertile hope that feminism may influence personal political attitude change among women.

Change in political behavior has been shown, however, to be the product of political attitude change of a second type as well: that related to system-focused political attitudes (Dennis 1975, 1976; Almond and Verba 1965; Sears and McConahay 1973; Gamson 1971, 1968; Forward and Wilson 1970; Flora and Lynn 1974; Schwartz 1973; Finifter 1973; Muller 1976). These relationships have been established with regard to both conventional and unconventional forms of political participation. The argument behind such research says, simply, that if individuals are to act politically, they must feel not only that personal action ought to be engaged in and can be effective, but also that the system can and will respond. Political attitudes dealing with the individual's perceptions of both personal political behavior and system responsiveness are involved in processes of changing political behavior. Both sets of political attitudes bear upon political behavior—and both are linked to feminist ideology.

FEMINIST IDEOLOGY AND POLITICAL ATTITUDES

Feminism provides an exceptionally appropriate vehicle for studying the relationship between ideology and political attitudes of both types just described. Not only does feminist ideology affirm activist personal political roles for women, but it posits faults in the system, rather than personal faults, as the explanation for women's relative lack of political power. In this way, feminist ideology is directly analogous to black power ideology in its implications for changes in political attitude.[3]

As the black activist rejects traditional stereotypes of blacks, so the feminist rejects stereotypical images of women as passive, submissive, politically uninterested, irrational, and so on (Riger 1977). Such negative stereotypes for both blacks and women can be seen as modifications to facilitate psychological adjustment to socially powerless positions and roles, and not as inherent or immutable character traits. Similarly, the social system and its persistent exclusion of blacks and women from the power centers of U.S. political, economic, and social life is blamed, rather than personal inadequacy, for low achievement by blacks and women as compared with white males.[4] Often, however, the perception that political and social demands are being ignored, sidetracked, or inadequately addressed leads to negative system affect—that is, political alienation among those so affected. As Pinard (1968) noted, there exist in the United States various large politically alienated subcultures that have negative evaluations of dominant cultural values and of the political system. Blacks in the United States have, historically, constitued one such subculture. Perhaps feminists constitute another.

The task of this part of the study is to assess how feminism affects the political attitudes of women. With the clear findings of Chapter 5 that feminism for men is differently structured, varies in content, and is not psychologically rooted as it is for women, the focus for the remainder of the study is only upon women. Men will be used as a comparison group only when comparative data can shed some helpful light upon the meaning of our findings about women.

Looking at all women as a group is clearly not the direction of analysis suggested by the last chapter, however. The one clear demographic characteristic that showed a surprising, strong, and essentially serendipitous relationship to feminism was race. Minority women were the only group where antifeminist views increased over time. While strongly more feminist than white women in 1972 (mean for white women = 72.9; mean for minority women = 88.2), that relationship was reversed by 1976 (mean for white women = 79.0; mean for minority women = 74.2). Even more perplexing was the finding that feminist support among black men during that time period rose markedly. (By 1976, the feminist mean for black men was a startling 92.6.) The primary explanation suggested for the findings among minority women, based on an item analysis, showed minority women's disenchantment with feminist views to occur in the areas of tactics, not in the areas of values or general perceptions of social reality. Nonetheless, it was clear that feminism was not functioning as a monolith among women. Black and other minority women were being affected by feminism differently than were white women. The obvious next question was, Did this also hold true for the relationship between feminism and political attitudes? Was the interaction between femaleness and minority race resulting in consistently different effects of and relationships to feminism?

Consequently, two primary categories of analysis were performed: analysis of changes in the relationship between feminism and political attitudes (1) over time and (2) by race. Several major questions were addressed: What is the direction of change in women's political attitudes over time? What is happening to the strength of the relationship between feminism and political attitudes over time? Does each of these phenomena differ when the sample is partitioned on the basis of race?

Specific hypotheses varied both in their complexity and their obviousness. (1) With all four personal political attitudes—political efficacy, political interest, protest approval, and citizen duty—a rise in means over time was expected. That is, it was anticipated that, if feminism had been successful in propagating its "new" notions of political roles for women, greater support for these attitudes should be evident. (2) The relationship between feminism and personal political attitudes was expected to strengthen—that is, regression coefficients should become higher. Whether, of course, this would be apparent with all personal political attitudes could not be anticipated. However, a trend toward a strengthening of these relationships was predicted. (3) With reference to system-focused attitudes, the expectation was that means would decline, indicating falling support for the political system and an increase in system-directed blame. (4) As with personal political attitudes, the relationship between feminism and system-focused attitudes was expected to strengthen. (5) For minority women, however, an alternative scenario was hypothesized. For reasons cited below, it was conjectured that, for black women, attitude change might be more intense than (and even, in some cases, in the opposite direction from) the changes in political attitude found among white women. (6) Furthermore, if our theory held, the relationship between feminism and political attitudes ought to be stronger among black women than among white women.

During the 1960s and very early 1970s, blacks of both sexes were experiencing increasing social consciousness of their placement and treatment within U.S. society. Awareness of relative deprivation on the part of minority groups was growing like the proverbial wildfire. In the late 1960s and early 1970s (before Nixon so ignominiously dismantled the Office of Economic Opportunity and other aspects of the war on poverty), blacks were also receiving tangible material gains at an unprecedented, if still not just, rate. Along with these gains came rising expectations.

By the mid-1970s, however, two major changers of consciousness had been on the scene for several years: feminism and Richard Nixon. Previous hopes for continued material gains were widely dashed under the Nixon presidency. In addition, notions that many minority women may have had in the early 1970s about both social structure and social change were subjected to major revision by feminism. Previous perceptions of U.S. society as racist, oppressive, discriminatory, and exploitative of blacks were now being compounded by awareness that the United States was sexist, oppressive, discriminatory, and exploitative of women as well. The United States was coming to be seen as characterized not only by racism and its resulting inhumanities, but also by sexism and its equally complex inequities. Where, then, did that leave minority women? Doubly oppressed, of course: oppressed by race, but also by sex.

Minority women's actually becoming more conscious of such double oppression would provide one plausible explanation for their reduced support of women's movement tactics and organization. Just as efforts aimed at ameliorating racial injustice did little, if anything, to offset problems of being female, so tactics aimed at lessening sex discrimination certainly did nothing to overcome problems of being black.

FEMINISM AND PERSONAL POLITICAL ATTITUDES

Change Over Time, 1972–76

Feminist emphasis on personal development, self-confidence, assertiveness, and involvement leads to the hypothesis that the level of personal efficacy, political interest, citizen duty, and protest approval (as indicated by mean scores on these variables) would rise during the period between 1972 and 1976. Table 6.1 presents slight but consistent support for this hypothesis for each of the four variables under investigation.[5] Indicators of how the individual perceived she could and ought to relate to the political system did strengthen over time.

But is this in any way actually related to feminism? Theoretically, an argument has been put forth. Feminism definitely attempts to influence sex-role perceptions in these areas, asserting the appropriateness and the desirability of women becoming more politically interested and effective, of their participating more in a variety of ways. Standard notions of citizen duty and approval of protest tap attitudes toward two such modes of participation—conventional and unconventional. If feminism is related to these attitudinal changes, multiple regression coefficients should indicate the strength of such relationships and show whether these relations have actually strengthened or weakened with time. Table 6.2 presents these findings,[6] and they are rather surprising.

Our overall hypothesis was given clear support. In each case but one, the relationship between feminism and the political attitude tested strengthened substantially with time. However, with reference to protest

TABLE 6.1: Mean Scores of Personal Political Attitudes of Women, 1972 and 1976

	1972	1976	Δ
Political efficacy	10.3	11.0	.7*
Political interest	6.2	6.9	.7*
Citizen duty	10.2	11.7	1.5*
Protest approval	6.9	7.8	.9*

*Significant at the .05 level.

Note: $\Delta = \overline{X}_{time\ 2} - \overline{X}_{time\ 1}$

Source: Compiled by the author.

TABLE 6.2: Comparison of Means on Personal Political Attitudes for White Women, Minority Women, and Minority Men, 1972 and 1976

	White Women			Minority Women			Minority Men		
	1972	1976	Δ	1972	1976	Δ	1972	1976	Δ
Political efficacy	8.0	11.0	3.0*	10.6	11.4	.8*	9.8	11.8	2.0*
Political interest	6.3	7.0	.7*	5.2	6.3	.9*	6.5	7.8	1.3*
Citizen duty	10.3	11.9	1.4*	10.0	10.3	.3	10.7	12.3	1.6*
Protest approval	8.2	7.5	-.7*	6.7	9.0	2.3*	8.9	8.7	-.2
	N = 546	N = 501		N = 83	N = 85		N = 42	N = 40	

*Significant at the .05 level.

Note: $\Delta = \overline{X}_{\text{time 2}} - \overline{X}_{\text{time 1}}$

Source: Compiled by the author.

approval, an initially strong relationship washed out. Thus, while approval of protest expanded among women overall, as indicated by the rise in means, this change does not relate directly to feminism. Rather, other cultural phenomena account for the rise in protest approval during this period.[7]

With reference to political efficacy, political interest, and sense of citizen duty, however, feminism *has* influenced political attitudes. Women's sense of political efficacy rose only slightly in the four-year period surveyed, but a marked increase occurred in the strength of the relationship between feminism and political efficacy. What is most striking, of course, is the unexpected negative sign of the regression coefficient. A rise in feminism was associated with a *decline* in sense of political efficacy—the opposite effect of the one hypothesized. The more feminist a woman is, the more likely she was *not* to feel politically efficacious. Are we finding that the disillusioned, those who feel most powerless to effect change in the system, are the ones most committed to feminist views? Is feminism appealing to politically alienated women by offering at least an explanation for their plight, even if not a viable hope or plan for altering it? Or are we seeing here that those women who try hardest to bring about change and to affect the political system are also the most likely to have experienced a sense of failure from their efforts? Are feminists generally feeling discouraged about the possibilities for affecting the system? Low political efficacy among feminists could reflect either view: (1) that the politically alienated are the ones who become feminists; or (2) that feminists have been trying within the political system and meeting with failure.

The latter possibility is made more disturbing when we note the strengthening relationship between feminism and political interest as well as between feminism and sense of citizen duty. In each case, women were becoming more, not less, system-oriented, as Table 6.1 showed. That feminism was strongly associated with these attitudes in 1976 but not in 1972 makes a clear and somewhat unsettling statement. By 1976, feminists are increasingly likely both to be politically interested and to feel a high sense of citizen duty. At the same time, they are *less* likely to believe that their political efforts will pay off. Feminists by 1976 are less hopeful about their potential political effectiveness than they were in the early 1970s!

Racial Differences in Personal Political Attitudes

Our next question is, How does race affect these relationships? Our findings are striking and quite consistent with the relative deprivation argument posited before. Changes in political attitudes of black women differed obviously from changes in those same attitudes among white women. These changes were also clearly different from the comparable changes found among black men. Race alone was clearly not the explanation for these differences. Minority race *combined with female sex*—the double obstacle—appears to be the obvious explanation here. Table 6.2 illustrates what has occurred.

As the third column in each section of this table indicates, the amount of change in each variable over time for each of the three subgroups represented shows clearly that minority women have changed in their personal political attitudes in a way quite different from that of white women, or of black men, for that matter. Where the sense of political efficacy among white women has shot up a substantial 3.0 over these four years (from a $\overline{X}$ of 8.0 to a $\overline{X}$ of 11.0), the gain for minority women is a meager .8. Even more striking is the fact that political efficacy among minority women in 1972 was substantially higher than it was for white women. Minority women experienced less than a third of the gain in political efficacy found among white women.

Most similar between the two groups of women are changes in political interest. While minority women have a lower mean than white women at both times, the amount and the direction of change is quite comparable for each group. Not so for a sense of citizen duty or for protest approval. Minority women have both a lower mean for and the smallest rate of increase in sense of citizen duty when compared both to white women and minority men. Their sense of obligation to the system, at least as reflected by attitudes toward voting, was markedly lower than that of white women. Even more striking was the finding that *only* among minority women did approval of protest rise over time—and it did so by a startling margin (see Figure 6.1).

For minority women by 1976, then, sense of efficacy and citizen duty were rising, but at a rate much lower than that for white women. Political interest was rising at a comparable rate between the two groups. But in marked contrast to the trend found among white women (and even among minority men), approval of protest had skyrocketed. For minority women, traditional forms of political participation seem essentially no more appealing than they did in 1972. Nontraditional forms of participation, such as those represented by political protest, however, have taken on markedly greater appeal.

But we still need to know the relationship between feminism and this phenomenon. Indeed, we need to know how feminism is related to each of these personal political attitude changes. Differences in these attitudes between whites and minority group members could be influenced by factors totally unrelated to feminism. Table 6.3, however, indicates that such is not the case. Feminism is related, and related strongly, to the personal political attitudes of minority women.

Most strikingly, feminism is more strongly associated with the political

FIGURE 6.1: Support for Protest Activity among White Women, Minority Women, and Minority Men, 1972–76

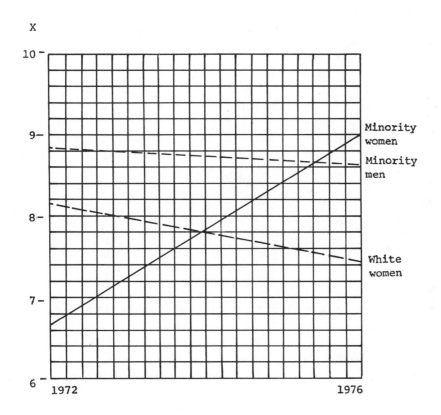

Source: Constructed by the author.

TABLE 6.3: Regression of Feminism with Personal Political Attitudes of White Women and Minority Women in 1972 and 1976

	White Women		Minority Women	
	1972	1976	1972	1976
Political efficacy	.03	−.08	.16	−.20*
Political interest	.12	.16*	.11	.17*
Citizen duty	.08	.11*	.13	.24*
Protest approval	.20*	−.08	.22*	.20*
	N = 543	N = 501	N = 83	N = 85

*Significant at the .05 level.
Note: Entries are betas.
Source: Compiled by the author.

attitudes of minority women for *each* personal attitude tested in 1976 than is true for white women. Feminism is affecting the personal political attitudes of minority women to a substantially greater extent than it is for white women. The strength of the negative relationship between political efficacy and feminism among minority women, combined with the strong rise among them in approval of protest, indicates that belief in the effectiveness of traditional as contrasted to nontraditional forms of political participation is waning sharply among this sector of the electorate. Feminist women of color are far more likely to support political protest in 1976 than in 1972 and less likely to believe that their traditional political efforts will be effective. Political alienation seems to be rising sharply among minority women.

FEMINISM AND SYSTEM-FOCUSED POLITICAL ATTITUDES

Feminism proffers a paradigm of social experience that argues that women's consistently subordinate roles and lesser power status in the economic, political, and social order are not the result of inherent personal or sex-based inadequacies, but, rather, result from the systems and structures in which women are forced to function. Increasingly, the political system has come under sharp attack from feminism as a source and perpetrator of inequality between the sexes. If feminism is succeeding at spreading its gospel then, as explained earlier, one would expect a decline in the means of those attitudes that imply support for the political system and strengthening of the relationship between feminism and these attitudes.

The system-focused variables studied were selected because they tapped a broad range of such political attitudes. Four variables, two individual items and two summed indices, provided directly comparable test questions in both years surveyed. The two individual items were political identification and pride in government. The two summed indices were scales for political trust and for perception of government attentiveness or responsiveness. For each variable, high scores indicated high or strong belief in the political system; low scores indicated the reverse.

Change Over Time

The first expectation, a decline in means for system-focused attitudes, was not supported by the findings (see Table 6.4). While pride in the government declined slightly and belief in government attentiveness dropped markedly, the means of the other two political attitudes tested actually rose. Hence, no clear pattern was evident.

Again, it was necessary to ask if feminism's relation to these attitudes over time was strengthening, regardless of the direction of change of the attitudes themselves. Table 6.5 provides some interesting (and, on the surface, contradictory) findings about these relationships. For instance, political community identification turned out not to be related to feminism at either time. Pride in the government was weakly related to feminism in 1972 but this relationship had disappeared by 1976. With each of the two stronger measures—stronger in the sense that they encompass several closely related items—virtually no relationship in 1972 changed into a moderately strong one in 1976. What at first appeared contradictory was that the signs on the coefficients for political trust and government attentiveness reversed. That is, as feminism rose, political trust fell and perception of government attentiveness rose. How could this be? Is this not grossly inconsistent?

These findings are not at all inconsistent. When we look at the individual items comprising each scale, we find clearly differing referents between the two variables. In the political trust index, items reflect trust of

TABLE 6.4: Mean Scores on System-focused Political Attitudes of Women, 1972 and 1976

	1972	1976	Δ
Political community identification	3.1	3.3	.2
Pride in government	4.4	4.1	−.3
Political trust	13.9	15.4	1.5*
Government attentiveness	15.2	11.5	−3.7*
	N = 629	N = 586	

*Significant at the .05 level.
Note: $\Delta = \overline{X}_{time\ 2} - \overline{X}_{time\ 1}$
Source: Compiled by the author.

TABLE 6.5: Regression of Feminism with System-focused Political Attitudes of Women, 1972 and 1976

	1972	1976
Political community identification	-.06	-.02
Pride in government	-.11[a]	.01
Political trust	-.00	-.19[b]
Government attentiveness	.04	.20[c]
	N = 629	N = 586

[a]Significant at the .05 level.
[b]Significant at the .01 level.
[c]Significant at the .001 level.
Note: Entries are betas.
Source: Compiled by the author.

the *people* currently running the government. In the government attentiveness index, on the other hand, referents are to parts of the political system. What seems to be happening among feminists is actually just what was anticipated. Although political trust by women generally is on the rise (Table 6.4), regression analysis showed that feminists are most likely to have low trust of *men* running the government. At the same time, feminists, by being more likely to believe the political system does pay attention to its citizenry, differ from women generally, whose sense of government attentiveness is on the wane.

Several rather obvious historical factors also may help explain such findings. For women generally, the period from 1972 to 1976 was marked by a change from the Nixon to the Ford presidency. It is no surprise that for the populace as a whole political trust during Ford's presidency was higher than it was during Nixon's era. Nor is it surprising that feminists' political trust would be declining particularly during this period. In 1972, the Equal Rights Amendment to the U.S. Constitution passed both houses of Congress by overwhelming margins. By 1976, however, opposition to the amendment was evident, formidable, and growing. In 1972, women may have believed they were being heard by the political system. By 1976, few such illusions were present. Feminists knew that over the past 20 years the pay gap between men and women had actually widened rather than narrowed[8] and that feminist demands had been evaded or ignored by politicians. Erosion of support for the Equal Rights Amendment, for daycare legislation, and for sexual preference rights were all vivid examples of this trend. Much of the political fluttering-of-wings over feminism was by 1976 recognized as symbolic rather than tangible, substantive commitment.

Explanations of why feminists saw the government as more attentive or responsive than did women generally are much harder to come by, however. Feminists in 1976 did believe the government was responsive. It is difficult to fathom why this was so. Perhaps the data indicate the strength of socialization or rationalization among white feminists—that is, that Americans live in a working democracy that will respond to needs of the people if only the people will express those needs clearly. Perhaps these data reflect a strong ambivalence on the part of white women, a feminist recognition that, indeed, all is not well, combined with a hesitance to blame the system itself for that flaw. After all, if the political system itself were seen to be at fault, then women would need to entertain the possibility either that change might be impossible within the existing system, or that the change required is so basic and major that it cannot be accomplished by the mere alteration of the few laws or the settlement of the few court cases upon which so many feminists pinned great hopes. Whatever the explanation, the finding is clear that feminists in 1976 perceived of the system as a whole, and in its specific parts, as attentive and responsive to people's demands.

Differences for White Women and Minority Women

But, again, we need to ask whether the results found hold equally for white and for minority women? Or does the compound relative deprivation hypothesis hold, showing minority women to be less system-supportive than are white women?

The data displayed in Table 6.6 show striking support for the deprivation hypothesis. In each of the four system-focused variables tested, black women showed strikingly different changes in political system support than was true for white women. With reference to political community identification, pride in government, and perception of government attentiveness,

TABLE 6.6: Comparison of Means of System-related Political Attitudes of White and Minority Women, 1972 and 1976

	White Women			Minority Women		
	1972	1976	Δ	1972	1976	Δ
Political community identification	2.9	3.4	.5*	3.2	3.0	-.2
Pride in government	3.6	4.2	.6*	4.5	3.3	-1.2*
Political trust	11.6	15.4	3.8*	14.3	15.1	.8*
Government attentiveness	12.9	11.9	-1.0*	15.6	9.7	-5.9*
	N = 543	N = 501		N = 83	N = 85	

*Significant at the .05 level.
Source: Compiled by the author.

minority women's support fell while that of white women rose. Political trust rose for both groups, but minority women experienced only one-fourth the rise in political trust found among white women.[9]

These findings become even more remarkable when we note that, for each variable, minority women had a higher mean than did white women (and higher, for that matter, than did minority men in three out of the four cases). Therefore, not only did minority women's support for the political system decline where that of white women's rose, but minority women also started from a higher point and fell to a lower one in all but one case.[10]

Furthermore, as Figure 6.2 illustrates clearly, this was not a race phenomenon alone. Black men did not show a comparable reversal in the trend of their political support. While the direction of change in perception of government attentiveness for minority men was similar to that found for minority women, the slope of the change was far less steep (see Figure 6.2). Political community identification of minority men began and remained higher than that for minority women. Minority men and white women both increased their pride in the U.S. government between 1972 and 1976. Minority women, on the other hand, experienced a notable drop in such pride. The rise in political trust for black men was almost equivalent to that of white women. In no way was the change in political trust among minority men comparable to the weak gain evidenced by minority women.

Clearly, minority women in 1976 were showing signs of political alienation not found among either white women or minority men. But is feminism related to this occurrence in any way? Is the decline in system support among minority women related to a compound sense of relative deprivation—that is, the awareness of racial deprivation associated with black consciousness combined with the awareness of sex-related deprivation associated with feminist consciousness?

Extremely interesting connections among race, feminism, and system-focused political attitudes are illustrated in Table 6.7. In 1972, when no relationship appeared to exist between white women's feminism and system-focused political attitudes, the political community identification and the government pride of black feminists was moderately strongly related—in a negative direction. That is, among minority women, who generally scored much higher on these two indicators of system support than did white women, feminism predicted low political community identification and low political trust. No such relationship held between feminism and political community identification in either year for white women.

For both groups of women, feminism predicted low trust and a higher than average perception of government attentiveness. But, again, the relationship found among minority women was stronger in each case than that found for white women. When one observes the change in coefficients for each group, it becomes clear that in each instance the change has been

FIGURE 6.2:   Change in Perception of Government Attentiveness among White Women, Minority Women, and Minority Men, 1972–76

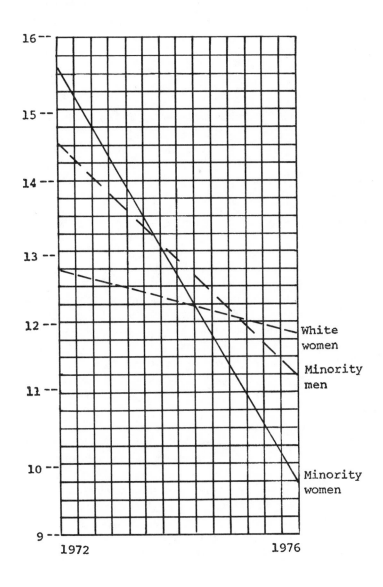

Note: Entries are mean scores.
Source: Constructed by the author.

TABLE 6.7: Regression of Feminism with System-focused Political Attitudes of White Women and Minority Women, 1972 and 1976

	White Women		Minority Women	
	1972	1976	1972	1976
Political community identification	−.02	−.02	−.29[b]	−.07
Pride in government	−.07	.01	−.22[a]	.01
Political trust	−.00	−.22[c]	.10	−.20[a]
Government attentiveness	.05	.14[a]	.11	.43[c]
	N = 543	N = 501	N = 83	N = 85

[a]Significant at the .05 level.
[b]Significant at the .01 level.
[c]Significant at the .001 level.
Note: Entries are betas.
Source: Compiled by the author.

greatest among minority women. Not only are these women showing clear signs of political disenchantment, but feminism is explaining more about this disenchantment for them than for white women. The relative deprivation hypothesis has been consistently and strongly supported.

But one last test remains. If minority women are feeling doubly oppressed—by sex as well as by race—then it should be seen that, by 1976, some portion of their discontent and anger was directed at the presidency and the federal government. The Nixon-Ford years saw a major dismantling of the antipoverty programs and benefits. Expectations of gains for blacks and women seem implied by the high support scores minority women registered in 1972. But by 1976 such hopes had clearly been dashed. Does the presidency and the federal government loom, then, as a direct target for blame by minority women?

The data in Table 6.8 respond with a resounding yes. While the mean evaluation of the federal government is only slightly lower among minorities than among whites in 1976 (3.9 versus 4.1, respectively), the relationship of this attitude to feminism is an obvious one—but *only* among minority women. Evaluations of the presidency were lowest among minority women (a mean of 3.7 compared with 4.6 for white women) and the strength of the relationship between feminism and presidential evaluation was striking. Virtually no relationship between feminism and presidential evaluation exists among white women, while such a relationship is very strong among black women.

The conclusion is clear. Feminism among minority women predicts governmental dissatisfaction. Minority women are not dissatisfied because they are black alone, but also because they are women and their feminism

TABLE 6.8: Regression of Feminism with Evaluations of the Presidency and the Federal Government among Minority and White Women in 1976

	Minority Women	White Women
Evaluation of federal government	-.17[a]	-.03
Evaluation of presidency	-.38[b]	.01
	N = 85	N = 501

[a] Significant at the .05 level.
[b] Significant at the .001 level.
Note: Entries are betas.
Source: Compiled by the author.

increases the extent to which they blame this political system for their condition within it. It appears as though the feminist consciousness of minority women may be markedly higher than the feminist consciousness of whites.

CONCLUSIONS

Several clear and important conclusions stand out from this part of the study. The level of political efficacy, political interest, citizen duty, and protest approval of women generally has risen between 1972 and 1976. Thus, our hypothesis that personal political attitude means of women would rise over time has been consistently and fairly strongly supported. Further, feminism is more strongly associated with these attitudes in 1976 than is true in 1972, with the important *caveat* that by 1976 feminism predicts a declining sense of political efficacy among women. Feminists are less likely than other women to believe that conventional political participation will be effective. Yet they are more likely to have high political interest and a high sense of citizen duty. Our second hypothesis, then, was also supported. Personal political attitudes *are* being affected by feminism to a greater extent in 1976 than in 1972.

Minority women's personal political attitude change differed markedly from that of white women. Feminism was strongly related to these attitudes. A sense of citizen duty and a sense political efficacy were both lower among minority women than among white women by 1976, but approval of protest had shot upward. Minority feminists were far more likely to support protest in 1976 than was true in 1972, and they were far more supportive of protest by 1976 than were white women. At the same time, minority feminists were least likely to believe in the efficacy of their conventional political participation, giving clear evidence of disenchantment with traditional system efforts at change among minority women.

With reference to system-focused political attitudes, results were less clear. No consistent decline in means for these variables was found when testing all women as a group. For minority women, however, a consistent and startling decline in these attitudes was documented. The relationship between feminism and those variables strengthened in two cases—political trust and government attentiveness—and weakened for pride in govern-ment. Importantly, feminism predicted a decline in political trust but a rise in perception of government attentiveness for both groups of women. This reflected a distrust of officials or persons running the government, while belief remained that the system itself could respond. Feminism also pre-dicted more about system-related political attitudes for minority women than for white women: feminism among minority women clearly predicted disatisfaction with the political system. The relative deprivation hypothesis posited for minority women was clearly supported.

Personal political attitudes among all women were found to be chang-ing, but the changes were in opposite directions for black women and for white women. Less clear change was evident among system-focused attitudes, when considering all women as a group, but a sharp consistent decline in such support was obvious among minority women. Feminism generally predicted a low sense political efficacy and low political trust for women. Neither white nor minority women saw the political system as more responsive in 1976 than in 1972.

White women seem most amenable to the kind of political attitude change that leads to behavioral change. White feminists have maintained relatively high belief in the system in spite of growing distrust of officials who run that system. Although it was true that the more feminist a white woman was, the more likely she was to feel a low sense of political efficacy, feminism did not predict approval of nontraditional political participation among whites. Rather, these women still saw traditional modes as viable.

Such was clearly not the case for feminism among minority women. Discouragement both with the political system and with personal ability to affect that system was glaringly evident among minority women. Feminism exacerbated both of these tendencies. Thus, it appears that minority women will be less likely to express political attitude changes of the personal sort that reflect sex-role changes. As Parsons and Bales (1955) contend, an alteration in role perceptions is most likely when supported either by growing public opinion or by actual social structure and incentives—that is, the role set as well as the role player generally needs to change. Attitude change toward roles usually implies both internal personal change and perceptions of external social change as well. Among minority women the latter change has clearly not occurred.

Among minority women, the low level of perception of the system as trustworthy, low level of support of traditional political participation, low evaluations of the federal government and the presidency, and high level of support for protest all combine to indicate that minority women do not see the role set—the political system—changing in ways conducive to their input and needs. If anything, the changes over time in the political attitudes of minority women show a growing perception of system intransigence and a rising sense of the futility of political effort—in short, political alienation.

How sadly ironic that those women who most direly need to have their condition improved feel least hopeful that either their own or the system's efforts are likely to bring about those needed improvements. How doubly ironic that sensitivity to the very ideology that aims to mobilize women that they may alter their social and political condition also seems directly related to making that condition appear all the more hopeless.

Yet, in another sense, what we see here is a strong, if somewhat twisted, indicator of exceptional success for feminist ideology. For, to the extent that feminism aims at consciousness-raising, at convincing women how far they have to go and how difficult is the fight, feminism has succeeded among black women to an extent not yet hinted at among whites.

NOTES

1. As Duverger said in his 1955 study of the political roles of women, it is "useless to give women a larger part in political life by special reforms. . . . The small part played by women in politics merely reflects and results from the secondary place to which they are still assigned by the customs and attitudes of our society and which their education and training tend to make them accept as the natural order of things. Purely political reforms are effective here only so far as they tend generally to modify this situation to counteract the effects of habit and tradition, to help women to free themselves from them, and to awaken them to a sense of their own independence. . . . It is probably still more important to fight against the deeply-rooted belief in the natural inferiority of women . . . a particularly serious obstacle because women feel deeply the special characteristics of their sex in this respect" (p. 130).

2. As Cochran (1972, pp. 24–25) describes it, "obviously for a time there will be two views of the role, the old and the new, perhaps in serious conflict and victory or suppression of the change will depend on the force of the institutional innovators in their personal relations and perhaps in the use of mass media and the power structure."

3. See Caplan (1970) for an extensive discussion of these aspects of black ideology.

4. See Cherniss (1972) and Sanger and Alker (1973) for verification of high system blame and rejection of stereotypical attitudes. Clearly, such notions were evident in the early feminist writings of Wollstonecraft, Susan B. Anthony, Elizabeth Cady Stanton, and Lucy Stone, as well.

5. Details concerning the content and coding of all scales are provided in Appendix B.

6. All regression equations included education, age, and liberal-conservatism as independent variables entered prior to the introduction of feminism in the equation. Thus, spurious effects of these variables (previously determined as significantly related to feminism) could not "muddy" the meaning of the coefficients by inflating them.

7. These data indicate that education now explains a moderate amount of the variance in

protest approval (beta of –.11), as does income and age (with betas of –.13 and –.14, respectively). That is, the less well educated, the lower the income, and the younger the age of the respondent, the more likely she or he is to approve of protest. Protest approval by 1976 in the United States shows moderate but consistent associations with age and socioeconomic class.

Studies of rise in protest approval among antifeminists have also been done recently. See Tatlock and Tedin (1978); also Brady and Tedin (1976).

8. These data and other scintillating statistics are reported in the March 1978 issue of the Project on the Status and Education of Women, Association of American Colleges, 1818 R Street, NW, Washington, D.C., 20009. They report that full-time female employees earned less than 59 cents for every dollar earned by men in comparable jobs, whereas 20 years ago, the ratio was 64 cents per dollar earned by men in comparable work. In addition, U.S. Labor Department statistics showed that salaries for traditionally female jobs are not keeping pace with salaries for traditionally male jobs.

9. The rise in means for white women was 3.8, compared with only .8 for minority women.

10. Richard Merelman (1973) argued for the existence of just such a phenomenon when he posited the predictability of lower political legitimacy among deprived and alienated subgroups of the culture.

7

FEMINISM AND POLITICAL PARTICIPATION

*T*he central theoretical assumption in the study of political ideology is that ideas affect behavior, that how and what an individual thinks can tell us something significant about a person's present or future behavior. While wide-ranging efforts in other disciplines such as psychology and sociology have argued that in certain circumstances many individuals first act and then think about or rationalize their past actions, political scientists have concentrated on tests of the opposite causal relationship between ideas and behavior (Ashford 1972; Converse 1964; Pye and Verba 1965; Adorno et al. 1950; Putman 1973; Wilker and Milbrath 1972; Pomper 1975; Nie et al. 1976). Studies of voting behavior, political psychology, political socialization, and political militancy all incorporate assumptions of linkages from ideology to behavior.

This study has been no exception to that rule. Rather, it undertook as its primary task a test of whether, in fact, ideas found within feminist ideology influence political behavior in measurable ways. Now is the time to take the last step in conducting that test and pull together, finally, the threads of the overall argument. Does feminist ideology actually make a difference in how women act toward the political system? That, after all, is what this study set out to discover.

This has been the argument of the study thus far. Political ideas and beliefs can influence behavior when they are integrated into a political belief system, an ideology. The likelihood that that ideology will influence personal political behavior is increased when the ideology has psychological meaning for the individual and exercises intellectual constraint upon the individual's thinking about related issues. The establishment of such an ideology within the individual is the first of three steps in the process of personal change that translates ideological belief into political behavior. The second requirement in the process is that the ideology effect political attitude change of both sorts, personal and system-focused, for the individual. Lastly, these changed political attitudes need to act as a catalyst for certain types of political behavior by the individual. If this sequence of effects occurs, then the argument that ideas influence behavior is supported.

We now find ourselves at the last point in that argument. Let us review quickly the terrain we have traveled to get here. First, feminism was argued to be a political ideology and was then empirically tested to determine whether it is. Chapter 3 described feminism as a belief system fulfilling the content requirements of a political ideology: statements describing reality, values and goal assertions, and proposals for social change. Empirical tests were then made to determine whether feminism gave evidence of constraint and of centrality in its belief structure. It did. Both theoretically and empirically, feminism qualifies as a political ideology.

Analyses were then run to see if feminism differed between men and women, especially with regard to its psychological linkages. Obviously and explicitly, feminism was expected to have a greater impact upon women than upon men, but it was necessary to see if there was any empirical basis for such an assumption. Indeed there was. Feminism was psychologically rooted for women, but not for men. The content of feminism varied between men and women, with women emphasizing values more than descriptive statements. The reverse was true for men. Furthermore, the actual structure of feminism ideology as represented by factor analysis was tighter for women than it was for men.

The potential for feminism to influence behavior, according to the argument of the study, was clearly present. The next step in determining whether this potential influence of ideology was actually operative (rather than being a mere fleeting dream-wish of research imagination) was taken in the last chapter—a test of whether feminist ideology influenced women's political attitudes. Again, the argument was obviously supported. Feminism was influencing political attitudes, both personal and system-focused, for American women. But one striking finding stood out within this research: feminism's effects upon political attitudes were clearly different for white women than for minority women. Race was compounding the effects of feminism in startling and remarkable ways.

The last test now remains. How does feminism influence the actual political behavior of American women?

To answer that question, the research design described in this chapter had to do several things. First, since racial effects of feminism upon political attitudes differed substantially, the argument of how ideology influences behavior predicts that the direct effects of ideology upon behavior will also differ from white women to minority women. Hence, the first part of the analysis looks at changes in the average level of various types of political participation for white and minority women from 1972 to 1976. The direct effects of feminist ideology upon each group are then investigated.

To leave the analysis at this point, however, would be to leave the argument only partially tested. Political attitudes have been argued to mediate the effects of ideology upon political behavior. If, in fact, attitudes function in that way, some effects of ideology upon behavior ought to be indirect. Indirect effects can not easily be measured by the forms of analysis used thus far, nor can the argument as a whole be examined rigorously in this manner. Thus, the second part of this chapter presents a causal model that illustrates the total theoretical argument of the research. This model is then examined by the use of path analysis, so that both direct and indirect effects of feminist ideology upon the political behavior of women can be measured and the argument tested as a whole. Since the political attitudinal effects of feminism differed so markedly by race, the analysis is carried out separately for white and for minority women and the results compared.

THE RELATIONSHIP OF WOMEN'S POLITICAL BEHAVIOR TO FEMINISM AND RACE

Gender role studies of the past have focused upon the less activist, less involved role of women in the political arena (Greenstein 1961; Jennings and Niemi 1971; Easton and Dennis 1969; Orum et al. 1974; Lynn and Flora 1973; Anderson 1975). Feminism aims directly to eliminate such gender role differences to whatever extent they exist. By affirming personal and political activism on the part of women, feminism encourages a broad range of political activity and supports both traditional forms of political participation, such as partisan, campaign, voting, and other electoral activities, and nontraditional forms of participation, such as protest, boycotts, demonstrations, sit-ins, and the like.

A variety of traditional gender role stereotypes and life situations most common to women have been postulated as inhibiting their political activism (Orum, et al. 1974; Lynn and Flora 1973; Andersen 1975; Hansen et al. 1976; Sapiro 1976; Welch 1977). Being a housewife and being a mother, for instance, have been singled out as particularly restraining influences upon women's involvement in the kinds of communication networks that enhance political interest and political group identity formation. Feminism aims directly at expanding and changing the communication networks of women. By so doing, feminism attempts to present models of alternative behavior, as well as alternative conceptual frameworks, for women to apply. Both the behavioral models and the conceptual frameworks have transference potential for women's political life.

Yet we have already found clear evidence that feminism does not have an equal impact upon all classifications of women. White and minority women clearly respond differently to feminism with regard to their political attitudes, as Chapter 6 sharply pointed out. These findings suggest, then, the hypothesis that the influences of feminism upon political behavior will show similar racial differences.

POLITICAL ALIENATION AND RACE

Literature on political alienation has consistently argued that a combination of positive perceptions of the political system provides the greatest potential for high levels of reform-oriented political activity (Schwartz 1973; Finifter 1973; Seligson 1977; Gamson 1968; Clarke 1973; Paige 1971; Aberbach 1969; Miller 1974). Finifter, Schwartz, and Miller each predict the highest levels of political participation among individuals with a high sense of political efficacy and a low sense of political trust. But, to date, only weak support (Miller 1976; Muller 1977; Paige 1971) for this hypothesis has been found in studies of actual political participation. While the data here did not show feminism among minority women to be related to a high sense of political efficacy (note the negative sign of the efficacy-feminism regression coefficients in Table 6.3), they did show feminism to be predictive of a high sense of political interest and citizen duty among women. In addition, feminism was also predictive of a falling sense of political trust in officials at the same time that minority feminists were experiencing a rise in their perception of the system's capacity to respond and a high sense of personal internal control.

Building upon the basic political alienation theory concerning participation, these data suggest an interesting modification of that theory. Distrust of officials running the political system was coupled with a basic belief both in the capacity of the system to respond and in a sense of personal competence (represented by the sense-of-internal-control index). If system variables are most important in predicting political behavior, perhaps it is the combination of low trust and high belief in the system as a whole that is the key combination for predicting political participation. If, on the other hand, some personal variable is crucial in this interaction, then perhaps it is a sense of internal control, more than a sense of political efficacy, that has something to tell us about likely political behavior. This latter possibility was tested as the final hypothesis, and requires a consideration of both direct and indirect effects of feminism upon the political participation patterns of white and of minority women.

HYPOTHESES

Based on the content of feminist ideology, the theoretical argument of the overall research, and the previous findings of the study, then, the testing of several hypotheses linking feminism and political behavior was obviously necessary to complete a full testing of the argument that political ideology influences political behavior:

1. Feminism should be more strongly associated with political participation of all women in 1976 than in 1972. The assumption here, of course, is that feminism has been measurably successful at effecting changes in political behavior among women during this time.
2. Because of their lower support for the political system, indicated by the means of political attitudes, and their lower overall education and income levels, minority women were expected to participate less politically than did white women.
3. Regardless of minority women's level of participation, however, the direct influence of feminism upon the political participation of minority women was expected to be stronger than it was for white women.
4. The total effects (direct plus indirect) of feminism upon political participation were expected to be stronger among minority than among white women.
5. High political participation among minority women was expected to be associated with low political trust and a high sense of internal control.

FEMINISM AND THE POLITICAL BEHAVIOR OF WOMEN IN 1972 and 1976

The first step testing the linkage between feminist ideology and political behavior was an investigation of the direct relationship between feminism and political participation of various types. A broad range of political participation was assessed with the 1972 and 1976 Survey Research Center (SRC) data—both conventional and nonconventional participation. Five measures of political participation of various types were developed for each respondent. Standard indicators of conventional electoral participation were used to measure campaign activity both (1) before and (2) after the presidential election. Thus, two traditional electoral behavior models were devised. A vote total score (3) was also composed for each respondent by summing the number of "did vote" responses on all five elections about which questions were asked. A local political participation score (4) was developed based on responses to questions that assessed involvement in local and community activities. The extent of political interest-group activity (5) was also measured for each respondent, as was *participation in protest* activities (6). For later use in the path model analysis, these six participation measures were also summed to yield a total political participation index for each person surveyed. Greater detail on the content and coding of the participation indices is provided in Appendix B.

The first question to be asked was whether the relationship between feminism and political participation become stronger in the four-year period studied. Between 1972 and 1976, we know, the mean feminism score for women rose from 74.0 to 78.2, as reported in Chapter 5. This rise in support for feminism was hypothesized to be an indication of a certain measure of success on the part of feminism in influencing political behavior as well. The findings of the last chapter that feminism was having a significant influence upon a broad range of political attitudes of both white and minority women lent further support to this assumption.

The findings here, however, lend only the weakest of support for this hypothesis. Table 7.1 dramatically illustrates this. While the relationship between feminism and both traditional campaign participation and political letter writing rises slightly, the change is weak and not significant. The general conclusion to be drawn from these data is, rather, that feminism is weakly but consistently related to the political participation of women and that this relationship has remained basically constant over the four-year period surveyed. Although feminism clearly was directly affecting political attitudes more in 1976 and in 1972, as Chapter 6 showed, such direct effects do not follow with reference to the political behavior of women.

But do white and minority women participate politically at a comparable rate? No; these data strongly supported the hypothesis that minority women would participate less politically than did white women. As Table 7.2 shows, on each of the six political participation measures tested, with the exception of interest-group activity, minority women participated politically less than white women. The single exception to this, interest-group activity, was surprising, however, given the generally low association between interest-group membership and being nonwhite that Verba and Nie (1972)

TABLE 7.1: The Relationship of Feminism to the Political Behavior of Women, 1972 and 1976.

Item	1972	1976
Traditional campaign participation	.14[c]	.17[c]
Vote total	.16[c]	.16[c]
Writing letters on political issues	.09[a]	.11[b]
	N = 629	N = 583

[a]Significant at the .05 level.
[b]Significant at the .01 level.
[c]Significant at the .001 level.
Note: Entries are betas.
Source: Compiled by the author.

TABLE 7.2: Comparison of Means of Political Behavior of White and Minority Women, 1976

Item	White Women	Minority Women
Preelection campaign activity	10.2	8.2*
Postelection campaign activity	14.5	11.9*
Vote total	11.4	8.8*
Local political participation	8.3	6.5*
Interest-group activity	12.5	14.0
Protest participation	3.4	3.3
Total political participation	60.4	52.7*
	N = 501	N = 82

*Differences in means signficant at the .05 level.
Source: Compiled by the author.

found. Further research into the nature of the groups to which minority women belong and how these relate to the political process seems both desirable and needed.

But the key question remains. How does feminism relate to political participation for women when race is taken into account? Do the effects of feminism differ significantly between white and minority women? The answer is a striking yes, and is reflected in the data presented in Table 7.3.

TABLE 7.3: Relationship between Feminism and Political Participation of Women in 1976, Partitioned by Race

	White Women		Minority Women	
Item	r	β	r	β
Preelection campaign activity	.07	-.03	.34[c]	.26[c]
Postelection campaign activity	.14[b]	.02	.29[b]	.21[a]
Vote total	.13[b]	.09	.27[b]	.19[a]
Local political participation	.16[b]	.04	.33[c]	.29[b]
Interest-group activity	.10[a]	.09	.12	.09
Protest participation	.13[b]	.06	.21[b]	.15
Total political participation	.19[b]	.07	.37	.28[b]
	N = 501		N = 82	

[a]Significant at the .05 level.
[b]Significant at the .01 level.
[c]Significant at the .001 level.
Source: Compiled by the author.

The relationship between feminism and political participation was consistently strong for minority women and consistently weaker among white women, as both the correlation and the regression coefficients presented indicate. Of particular note, in light of the last chapter's findings of political disenchantment among minority women, was the finding that feminism does, in fact, relate strongly to the traditional political activity of minority women. The moderate relationship found between feminism and voting was not surprising given other research findings that suggest that voting is a relatively easy and expected political act for women, and one not strongly influenced by gender-role differences or egalitarian attitudes (Lansing 1974; Sapiro 1976; Andersen 1975). What was most surprising, however, was the finding that the relationship between feminism and protest activity was not stronger. The findings of the previous chapter had led us to expect that feminist black would engage in more protest activity than would nonfeminist blacks, and this truns out not to be the case. Instead, these data show that, while feminism is related strongly to approval of protest among minority women, such political attitudes had not by 1976, been translated into actual political behavior to any great extent.[1]

Table 7.4 lends additional evidence to this finding by showing the consistently stronger relationship among minority women between feminism and single indicators of traditional political participation. In all but one instance, feminism was found to be moderately strongly related to the political participation of minority women but not of white women.

FEMINISM PLUS MINORITY-GROUP MEMBERSHIP HEIGHTENS POLITICAL ALIENATION

What, then, does all this imply about political alienation among minority women? We have found now that American women of color participate markedly less than do their white counterparts, but that feminism is far more influential in getting them to participate than is true among white women. We are also reminded, from earlier discussion, that individuals' need to feel personally competent in the political arena before they will engage in political activity has strong theoretical support (Verba and Nie 1972; Almond and Verba 1965; Campbell et al. 1964; Pomper 1975; Verba, Nie, and Petrocik 1976). Yet this relationship did not hold for minority women in this study.

POLITICAL EFFICACY

Several previous findings are directly related to the question of political alienation among minority women and need to be made explicit before the

TABLE 7.4: Regression of Feminism with Traditional Political Participation of White and Minority Women, 1976

Item	White Women	Minority Women
Registered	.02	.18*
Did campaign work	−.02	.20*
Contributed money to campaign	−.06	.12
Had congressional contact	−.07	.20*
Tried to convince others	.09	.20*
Wrote about political issue	.01	.21*
Worked on local issues	.06	.26*
Made contribution on local issue	.06	.18*
	N = 501	N = 82

*Significant at the .05 level.
Source: Compiled by the author.

question can be answered more fully. First, minority women overall experienced a slight rise in their sense of political efficacy between 1972 and 1976 (see Table 6.2). Yet the relationship between feminism and sense of political efficacy dropped markedly within the same period. By 1976, the higher the feminism score of minority women, the greater were the chances of their having a *low* sense of political efficacy. Furthermore, a sense of political efficacy has been associated traditionally with demographic variables reflective of high socioeconomic status (Verba and Nie 1972; Pomper 1975). The analysis of these data has shown quite clearly that different relationships exist between feminism and demographic variables depending upon the race of the respondent. As Table 7.5 clearly illustrates, demographic factors are far more related to the feminism of white women than is true for minority women. In fact, for minority women, family income turns out to be virtually unrelated to feminism, social class to be inversely related to feminism, and youth to be much less predictive of feminism. Feminism among white women is far more directly connected to socioeconomic factors than is true for minority women. Minority women often are feminist in spite of, not because of, their social class standing.

Feminism among minority women cuts across social class lines. Among white women, feminism can be argued to be largely a matter of middle-class consciousness, with white women identifying primarily with men in their social class and seeing themselves comparatively worse off.

What this says about the meaning of feminist ideology between the races is profound. On the one hand, feminism among white women seems to act as a focus for a sense of "fraternal" deprivation, while for minority women, feminism appears to function as a lens magnifying their sense of absolute deprivation.

TABLE 7.5:   Regression of Feminism and Demographic Variables for White and Minority Women, 1976

	White Women		Minority Women	
	r	β	r	β
Marital status	.23*	.14*	.06	.08
Employment status	.15*	.07	.02	−.05
Having children	−.11*	.04	.02	.06
Age	−.33*	−.18*	−.12	−.00
Subjective social class	.12*	.04	−.14	−.18*
Education	.34*	.18*	.21*	.24*
Family Income	.23*	.12*	.02	−.06
		$r^2 = .44$		$r^2 = .28$
	N = 501		N = 82	

*Significant at the .05 level.
Note: Betas are from multivariate regression analysis.
Source: Compiled by the authors.

How is this conclusion supported? For white women, feminism was largely a function of socioeconomic factors. Demographic variables accounted for nearly half of all the variance in the feminism index for white women ($r^2 = .44$). Being unmarried, young, childless, well educated, and a member of a family with high income strongly predicted being feminist for white women. Thus young, middle- and upper-middle-class women make up the bulk of support for feminism among whites. These white women—not economically deprived by objective poverty standards—are the ones most inclined to feel discriminated against and unequally treated, that is, subject to sexism. Comparing themselves, in all probability, to where men with comparable education find themselves in terms of money, jobs, political power, and so on, these women feel that as a group they are unfairly treated. A sense of fraternal deprivation appears to exist among white feminists, probably coupled with rising expectations for justice and equality as a natural product of their higher education.

Feminism among blacks, on the other hand, functions quite differently, being explained far less by demographic variables. Several clear differences stand out. For one, age has virtually no relationship with feminism for minority women. Rather, minority women of all ages are equally likely to be feminist. Strikingly, the relationship between income and feminism disappears among minority women, while it remains strong among whites. Furthermore, the relationship between social class perception and feminism is an *inverse* one among minority women. That is, the lower the social class a minority woman considered herself to be in, the *more* likely she was to be feminist—not the other way around as was true among white women.

Minority women are more likely to be members of the lower class than of the middle class. Black feminism is clearly not dominated by social class and age in the same way that feminism among white women is.

Aspiration levels among the two groups of women may also explain some of the difference in feminism and the kind of deprivation it highlights. For white women, learned aspiration levels are consistently higher than for blacks. It is not surprising, then, that the higher the education and general socioeconomic standing of white women, the more they expect and believe they ought to have; hence, the more easily they may become dissatisfied and indignant. The higher the status of white women, the more likely feminism is to be channeled into the sense of relative fraternal deprivation that they feel.

Yet aspiration level works differently among minority women. Traditionally taught through both formal learning and awareness of reality that they are likely to achieve less than whites or black men, minority women who advance above the average and relatively low level of other minority women may well believe they have exceeded realistic (but not necessarily just) expectations. To the extent that this is the case, minority women as they rise in socioeconomic standing compared to other minority women might be less likely to support feminism for fear of what they might lose. If their reference group is other minority-group members, especially women, their gains in relation to their learned expectations may make it seem that discrimination is less rampant than it appears to those women still on lower rungs of the social and economic ladder. Having made it, in terms of economic success, can act as a real retardant to awareness of inequities.

An observer of black feminists cannot (unlike an observer of white feminists) say, "the more they have, the more they expect." Minority women experience far more actual deprivation in material objective terms than do white women, as evidenced by the undeniable differences in average family income and education found earlier. The sense of deprivation feminism heightens among these women appears not to be relative fraternal deprivation but rather a sense of deprivation when comparing one's self to all other Americans. The sense of deprivation represented by the relationship of feminism to socioeconomic factors occurs among minority women regardless of, and not because of, their social and economic standing within their racial group.

Feminism, for all women who support its ideology, draws attention to inequality and injustice, to oppression, and to discrimination of various forms. But feminist ideology appears to represent different things to different women. Among minority women, feminism appears to be interpreted in light of absolute deprivation. Among white women, on the other hand, the interpretation of reality feminism proffers appears to be one of relative fraternal deprivation.

THE TRUST-EFFICACY COMBINATION

But this discussion of the differences existing in the relationship between feminism and socioeconomic factors for minority women and for white women was undertaken to explain the unexpectedly low sense of political efficacy found with high political participation among minority women and not the low trust, high efficacy combination argued for by the Gamson alienation hypothesis. Is this theory of political alienation basically incorrect when applied to members of minority groups?

The theory is probably not incorrect for minority-group members. Rather, it seems more plausible to argue that a modification of the theory is in order than to say that the theory simply is incorrect. What Schwartz, Finifter, and others argue, essentially, is that the combination of feeling able to affect the political system and being dissatisfied with that system is the crucial combination for political participation. If we feel capable of effecting change and see no need for change (high efficacy, high trust), we have little reason to act, they argue. If we feel the need for change, but also feel we cannot bring change about (low trust, low efficacy), we are also unlikely to act politically. Clearly, if we feel both that no change is needed, and that even if it were we could do little that would be effective to bring about change (high trust, low efficacy), we are least likely to act. Thus, there is high theoretical plausibility in the basic theory itself. Low trust and high efficacy do seem, potentially, to be the most likely combination to motivate political behavior. Why, then, does this combination not hold in the strong relationship between feminism and the political participation of minority women?

Perhaps it is because sense of political efficacy is the wrong variable to focus upon for the theory. As Weissberg (1973), Seligson (1977), and Jacob (1971) each showed, the validity of the sense-of-political-efficacy measure is open to question. Exactly what this is a measure of is not clearly agreed upon. What is essential to the alienation theory, however, is the idea that a sense of personal effectiveness must be present to give the individual the hope he or she needs to act. That is, if one feels personally ineffective, so that efforts toward change one initiates seem doomed, then one is not likely to act. A reasonable hope of success is essential to motivate action.

The measures of (1) a sense of internal control and (2) a sense of government attentiveness or responsiveness may very well measure that hope of success. Perhaps it is the combination of low trust and high sense of internal control that is crucial, either in and of itself or combined with a sense of government responsiveness. Exactly this combination of low trust in officials, high sense of internal control, and strong belief in government responsiveness was found in the political attitudes associated with feminism among minority women.

CAUSES OF WOMEN'S POLITICAL PARTICIPATION

The next, and final, analysis to be performed involves the more complex technique of causal path analysis. Thus far, we have used simple cross tabulations, comparisons of means, simple correlation, and multivariate regression. Path analysis is, basically, an extension of correlation and regression analysis, but one whereby more than one dependent variable can be dealt with at once. In the analyses presented previously, only one dependent variable, such as political trust or approval of protest was investigated at a time. In causal analysis, hypotheses and models can be tested that involve a series of variables that can be related to one another in several ways. For example, in path analysis, the combined effects of social class on political participation may be tested at the same time that effects of social class upon feminism, political efficacy, and other variables are also being studied.[2] Before presenting this analysis, a few words are in order about the technique itself and the variables used here.

First, causal analysis does not *prove* causality. Rather, it strengthens the basis upon which one may make inferences, and it allows various hypotheses to be tested and summarized in a statistical model. The researcher focuses upon what appear to be the principal causes for some phenomenon and assumes, thereby, the direction of the relationship between those variables. The relationships themselves are indicated in an abstract model based upon the theory or theories the researcher is investigating. Obviously, then, not all possible causal influences are tested, but only those being scrutinized because of some theoretical framework. Generally, only the most central factors are tested. Results of the investigation then allow predictions about what is likely to occur under certain conditions. The accuracy of these predictions, tested in other instances, leads to modification or retention of the model, all of which contributes to the building of theory in the field.

Causal analysis, however, is more a panacea for research on political science than is any other single research technique in any other discipline. Certain critical and at times questionable characteristics are inherent in the technique. For instance, causation is assumed to be one-directional rather than reciprocal or two-way. The researcher must make a prior decision on the direction of causality in the relationship between any two variables. In this study, for instance, it is assumed that feminism influences political attitudes and political behavior and not the other way around. It is quite possible, however, that in certain political circumstances a woman's political behavior could be met with such unaccepting male response that her feminism would be heightened, but this study does not presume that as a rule an individual's feminism is produced by her political behavior.

The model used employs all the major variables studied in preceeding chapters and, thus, serves as a summary of that work. The model allows measurement of the relative strength of the different variables, and of relationships in terms of the ultimate dependent variable, political participation. In this way, the proportionate effect of each variable is assessed so that direct, indirect, and total combined impacts are measured in some way. This method, therefore, provides several advantages to the research. It conveniently summarizes complex relationships around several variables. Through being tested with two subgroups, white women and minority women, the method allows us to assess how relatively stable or fluid particular variables are as influences upon political behavior.

The analysis thus far has not examined the overall theoretical model of the relationship between feminist political ideology and political behavior. The impact of feminist ideology upon political attitudes has been assessed directly, as have the direct effects of feminism upon political behavior. But more is needed. No clear connections, for example, have yet been established between feminism and political participation through political attitudes.

A recursive path model of presumed important influences on the political participation of women over time is presented in Figure 7.1.[3] Obviously, chronology is assumed here as one of the justifications for the theoretical structure of the model. It can reasonably be assumed that demographic or sociological characteristics such as one's age, education level, socioeconomic standing, and party identification usually exist before one's ideological stance is developed. Socioeconomic status largely has been determined for individuals by the existing social structure and the life opportunities available to them. Similarly, the other exogenous variable in the model, political party identification, is assumed to be a product of childhood and early adult socialization; it is further assumed that it is not likely to change significantly within the relatively short time span (four years) of this study. Indeed, comparisons of means of party identification show this to be a valid assumption (mean party identification in 1972 is 3.5; in 1976 3.6).

The next assumption in the model is that ideological and psychological belief sets, such as one's liberalism-conservatism, feminism, and sense of internal control, are widely encompassing belief systems that are the product of one's general life situation, and that these belief sets have clear and often strong influences on more specific political attitudes, later variables in the causal sequence. While not a political ideology, the sense of internal control has been found to be a strong influence upon the nature of specific political attitudes (Riger 1977; Sanger and Alker 1973; Rotter 1966; Forward and Williams 1970). The sense of internal control is expected, therefore, to function within the causal model in a manner similar to political ideology. Party identification, age, and socioeconomic standing are perceived as contributing to the development of these three belief sets.

FIGURE 7.1 Direct Effects of Political Participation of Women

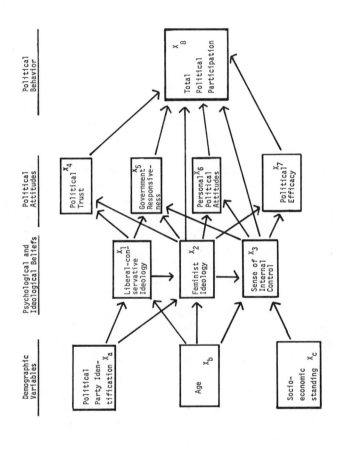

Source: Compiled by the author.

Once an opportunity for political behavior presents itself, then, the presumption of the model is that political attitudes will be the strongest predictor of the kind and frequency of political activity in which the individual engages. Yet these influences upon political behavior are concomitantly assumed to be influenced by the preceding variables within the causal sequence. The path model simply presents, in a manner amenable to rigorous empirical testing, a visual image of the social process believed to influence political behavior.

HYPOTHESES

The basic hypotheses being investigated are that (1) political attitudes will be the strongest predictor of the political behavior of women; (2) feminism will positively predict political behavior (that is, the higher the feminism score of women, the more likely they will be to participate politically); (3) the predictive strength of feminism will be markedly stronger for the political participation of minority women than for that of white women; and (4) socioeconomic status will be a stronger influence upon the political participation of white women than upon that of minority women.

The ordering of the variables is important since it reflects the assumption of one-way causation.[4] Variables placed early in the model are assumed to be unaffected by those variables that appear later. The presented ordering is that which is most logical and generally accepted given other research and theory in the field.

After the variables are ordered within the model, a series of multiple regressions assessed the impact of each one. This measure is the "path coefficient," which is statistically equivalent to the beta weights used earlier. These coefficients are placed on the "paths" in the model (see Appendix B). Their derivation involves a two-step process. First, every possible relationship between the variables contained in the model is assessed by regression analysis, and all relationships that are below statistical significance are dropped. Secondly, each remaining variable in the path model is treated as a dependent variable in multiple regression, and beta weight (path coefficients) are computed for all variables having a single direct path to each particular dependent variable. This process is complicated, of course, by the fact that we are dealing not only with one but, rather, with a series of dependent variables. Tables 7.6 and 7.7 present the decomposed effects of the various variables upon the political participation of white and minority women.

POLITICAL PARTICIPATION PATHS FOR WOMEN

As Figure 7.1 indicated, the causal model proposed two sets of political attitudes as directly influencing political participation—personal political

TABLE 7.6: Decomposition of Effects on Political Participation of White Women, 1976

Dependent Variable	Predetermined Independent Variable	Total Association r	Direct Effect β	Indirect Effects via							Total Effects
				x_1	x_2	x_3	x_4	x_5	x_6	x_7	
Liberal-conservative ideology (x_1)	x_a (PID)	.20	.20	—	—	—	—	—	—	—	.20
	x_b (Age)	.11	.10	—	—	—	—	—	—	—	.10
	x_c (Socioeconomic Status)	-.02	-.03	—	—	—	—	—	—	—	-.03
Feminism (x_2)	x_a	-.05	-.11	-.02	—	—	—	—	—	—	-.13
	x_b	-.33	-.26	.01	—	—	—	—	—	—	-.25
	x_c	.31	.26	-.06	—	—	—	—	—	—	.19
	x_1	-.17	-.12	—	—	—	—	—	—	—	-.12
Internal control (x_3)	x_a	.16	.09	—	-.01	—	—	—	—	—	.08
	x_b	-.08	.02	—	-.02	—	—	—	—	—	.00
	x_c	.35	.34	—	.02	—	—	—	—	—	.36
	x_2	.14	.06	—	—	—	—	—	—	—	.06
Political trust (x_4)	x_a	.08	.06	.01	-.02	.00	—	—	—	—	.05
	x_b	.01	-.07	.00	.05	.00	—	—	—	—	-.02
	x_c	-.04	-.02	.00	-.05	.01	—	—	—	—	-.06
	x_1	.08	.04	—	-.03	—	—	—	—	—	.01
	x_2	-.20	-.21	—	—	.01	—	—	—	—	-.20
	x_3	.02	.04	—	—	—	—	—	—	—	.04
Government responsiveness (x_5)	x_a	.01	-.05	.01	-.01	.01	—	—	—	—	-.04
	x_b	-.12	-.04	.01	-.04	.00	—	—	—	—	-.07
	x_c	.22	.13	-.00	.03	.05	—	—	—	—	.20
	x_1	.03	.05	—	.02	—	—	—	—	—	.03
	x_2	.20	.13	—	—	.01	—	—	—	—	.14
	x_3	.21	.15	—	—	—	—	—	—	—	.15

(continued)

117

TABLE 7.6 (continued)

Dependent Variable	Predetermined Independent Variable	Total Association r	Direct Effect β	Indirect Effects via							Total Effects
				x_1	x_2	x_3	x_4	x_5	x_6	x_7	
Personal political attitudes (x_6)	x_a	.06	-.02	.01	-.02	.01	—	—	—	—	-.02
	x_b	-.01	.13	.01	-.04	.00	—	—	—	—	.10
	x_c	.33	.28	.00	.04	.04	—	—	—	—	.36
	x_1	.03	.05	—	.02	—	—	—	—	—	.03
	x_2	.22	.17	—	—	.01	—	—	—	—	.18
	x_3	.24	.13	—	—	—	—	—	—	—	.13
Political efficacy (x_7)	x_a	.09	.03	.01	.01	.02	—	—	—	—	.06
	x_b	-.05	-.02	.01	.04	.00	—	—	—	—	.03
	x_c	.20	.15	.00	.02	.01	—	—	—	—	.18
	x_1	.04	.01	—	.01	—	—	—	—	—	.02
	x_2	-.00	-.08	—	—	.01	—	—	—	—	-.07
	x_3	.22	.18	—	—	—	—	—	—	—	.18
Total political participation (x_8)	x_a	.08	.01	.00	-.01	.00	-.00	.00	.01	.00	.01
	x_b	-.08	-.02	.00	-.01	.00	.00	.00	.05	.00	.03
	x_c	.35	.16	-.00	.01	.02	.00	-.00	.11	.02	.32
	x_1	.02	.01	—	-.00	—	.00	.00	.00	.00	.01
	x_2	.19	.03	—	—	.00	.01	.00	.07	.01	.12
	x_3	.23	.05	—	—	—	-.00	.00	.05	.02	.12
	x_4	-.10	-.05	—	—	—	—	—	—	—	-.05
	x_5	.22	-.02	—	—	—	—	—	—	—	-.02
	x_6	.50	.41	—	—	—	—	—	—	—	.41
	x_7	.19	.10	—	—	—	—	—	—	—	.10

$r^2 = .55$

Note: N = 501.
Source: Compiled by the author.

TABLE 7.7: Decomposition of Effects on Political Participation of Minority Women, 1976

Dependent Variable	Predetermined Independent Variable	Total Association r	Direct Effect β	Indirect Effects via							Total Effects
				x_1	x_2	x_3	x_4	x_5	x_6	x_7	
Liberal-conservative ideology (x_1)	x_a (PID)	.23	.24	—	—	—	—	—	—	—	.24
	x_b (Age)	.11	.11	—	—	—	—	—	—	—	.11
	x_c (Socioeconomic status)	-.04	-.01	—	—	—	—	—	—	—	-.01
Feminism (x_2)	x_a	-.11	-.10	-.06	—	—	—	—	—	—	-.16
	x_b	-.12	-.10	-.03	—	—	—	—	—	—	-.13
	x_c	.08	.04	.00	—	—	—	—	—	—	.04
	x_1	-.26	-.23	—	—	—	—	—	—	—	-.23
Internal control (x_3)	x_a	-.07	-.11	—	-.02	—	—	—	—	—	-.13
	x_b	-.10	.09	—	.02	—	—	—	—	—	.11
	x_c	.31	.36	—	.01	—	—	—	—	—	.37
	x_2	.23	.21	—	—	—	—	—	—	—	.21
Political trust (x_4)	x_a	.36	.38	-.03	.01	.00	—	—	—	—	.36
	x_b	.28	.30	-.01	.01	.00	—	—	—	—	.30
	x_c	-.10	.03	.00	-.00	-.01	—	—	—	—	.02
	x_1	.03	-.12	—	-.03	—	—	—	—	—	-.09
	x_2	-.18	-.13	—	—	.01	—	—	—	—	-.14
	x_3	-.10	-.03	—	—	—	—	—	—	—	-.03
Government responsiveness (x_5)	x_a	-.08	-.02	.01	-.04	-.02	—	—	—	—	-.07
	x_b	-.17	-.17	.01	-.04	.02	—	—	—	—	-.18
	x_c	.06	-.11	-.00	.02	.07	—	—	—	—	-.02
	x_1	-.08	.05	—	-.09	—	—	—	—	—	-.04
	x_2	.43	.38	—	—	.04	—	—	—	—	.42
	x_3	.26	.19	—	—	—	—	—	—	—	.19

(continued)

TABLE 7.7 (continued)

Dependent Variable	Predetermined Independent Variable	Total Association r	Direct Effect β	Indirect Effects via							Total Effects
				x_1	x_2	x_3	x_4	x_5	x_6	x_7	
Personal political attitudes (x_6)	x_a	-.49	-.48	.02	-.02	-.01	—	—	—	—	-.49
	x_b	-.12	-.11	.01	-.02	.01	—	—	—	—	-.11
	x_c	.02	-.02	-.00	.01	.03	—	—	—	—	.02
	x_1	-.09	.10	—	-.02	—	—	—	—	—	.08
	x_2	.29	.23	—	—	.01	—	—	—	—	.24
	x_3	.16	.07	—	—	—	—	—	—	—	.07
Political efficacy (x_7)	x_a	.20	.19	-.02	.02	.01	—	—	—	—	.20
	x_b	-.06	.01	.01	.02	-.01	—	—	—	—	.03
	x_c	.13	.15	-.00	-.01	-.03	—	—	—	—	.11
	x_1	-.01	-.09	—	.04	—	—	—	—	—	-.05
	x_2	-.17	-.16	—	-̇	-.02	—	—	—	—	-.18
	x_3'	-.08	-.08	—	—	—	—	—	—	—	-.08
Total political participation (x_8)	x_a	-.30	.04	-.02	-.01	-.02	-.05	-.00	-.23	.00	-.29
	x_b	-.19	.01	.01	-.01	.02	-.04	-.03	-.05	.00	-.09
	x_c	.16	.06	.00	.00	.07	.00	-.02	-.01	.00	.10
	x_1	-.18	-.10	—	-.02	—	.02	.01	.05	-.00	-.04
	x_2	.37	.06	—	—	.04	.02	.07	.11	.00	.30
	x_3	.36	.19	—	—	—	.02	.04	.03	-.00	.28
	x_4	-.34	-.14	—	—	—	—	—	—	—	-.14
	x_5	.38	.19	—	—	—	—	—	—	—	-.19
	x_6	.60	.48	—	—	—	—	—	—	—	.48
	x_7	-.08	.01	—	—	—	—	—	—	—	.01
			$r^2 = .72$								

Note: N = 85.
Source: Compiled by the author.

120

attitudes and system-focused political attitudes. Initially, those variables presented earlier (Chapter 6) in the personal political attitude group were simply summed; a composite score for each respondent was used in the equations. It soon became apparent, however, that the negative sign of the political efficacy variable clouded the effects upon political participation both of political efficacy and of the remaining three variables (political interest, citizen duty, and protest approval), each of which had a positive sign. Consequently, political efficacy was run separately in the equations and the single summed score of the remaining three personal political variables included in equations as the variable referred to as "personal political attitudes."

It was not assumed that there were any reciprocal interactions among any of the political attitude variables, because there was no clear theoretical reason for doing so. The model is not, therefore, testing the existence of such interactions. It is simply presuming that none exist.

Now let us first consider the major effects presented in Table 7.6 Although a fairly powerful r-squared of .55 was achieved by the final model equation (based on direct effects only), we see that explanatory power resulted essentially from two variables. Personal political attitudes and socioeconomic factors accounted for half the variance in the political participation of white women in 1976. When we move to the last column to study total effects of each variable upon political participation, however, we note several additional findings. First, the decomposition of effects has yielded indirect effects that actually double the influence of socioeconomic standing upon white women's political participation. In addition, the indirect effects of feminism and of internal control now make each of these variables significant but comparatively weak predictors of political participation. A simple illustration of significant predictors of the political participation of white women is presented in Figure 7.2.

As anticipated, the picture we find for black women differs substantially from that found for white women, as Figure 7.2 portrays. First, the final multiple regression equation among the minority subsample yielded a startling r-squared of .72. Of the total variance in the political participation of minority women, 72 percent was explained by this model. Direct effects upon political participation showed personal political attitudes, again, to be the primary predictor of political behavior, with sense of government responsiveness and internal control the next strongest influencers. When we move to the total effects column, however, some significant and striking changes in the comparative influence of the variables upon political participation stand out. Feminism has become the second strongest effector of minority participation. Political party identification and sense of internal control now follow closely. Each of these three variables has strong indirect effects upon political participation that ordinary multivariate analysis is not able to discern.

FIGURE 7.2: Significant Influences on the Political Participation of Women, 1976 (total effects)

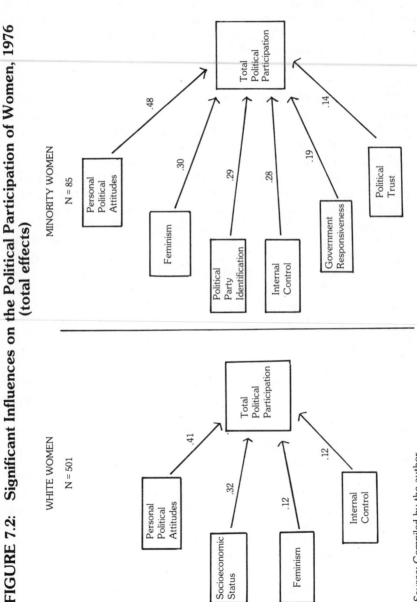

WHITE WOMEN

N = 501

MINORITY WOMEN

N = 85

Source: Compiled by the author.

The basic hypotheses being tested with reference to political participation have received strong support. Political attitudes *are* the strongest predictor of women's political participation. This is true for white women and for minority women. In both cases, however, the personal political attitudes of citizen duty, political interest, and approval of protest are far stronger influences upon political participation than are the system-related political attitudes. Only among minority women do system-related attitudes show a strong influence upon political participation, a finding discussed in more detail below.

FEMINISM'S INFLUENCE UPON WOMEN'S POLITICAL BEHAVIOR

Feminism was a significant predictor of the political participation of both subgroups, but weakly so for white women, strongly so for minority women. Socioeconomic factors were also found to be strongly predictive of white political participation and insignificantly predictive of minority participation. All four hypotheses tested were given strong support.

Far more was unearthed in this analysis, however, than this brief discussion indicates. Other racial differences in the political participation of women stand out. Socioeconomic standing is a powerful influence on white women's political participation both directly and indirectly, but a very weak influence on that of blacks.[5] Conversely, political party identification was a far more powerful influence upon the political participation of minority women than was true for white women, and substantially more powerful than was expected theoretically.[6]

Interestingly, low political trust definitely did heighten political participation—but only among minority women. These data showed that minority women who participate above the norm tend to be characterized by a low level political trust, a high sense of internal control, and a high perception of government responsiveness. In relation to the earlier discussion of political alienation theory, it may well be that this combination is the crucial one for positively influencing political activism.

Strikingly, we note that for both subsamples the influence of feminist ideology upon political participation is greater than the influence of traditional liberal-conservative ideology. Feminism does influence political participation, but it does so differently for white women and for minority women. For both groups, the effects of feminism are primarily indirect, through political attitudes. Upon minority women, feminism exercises another indirect influence on participation, through internal control. Among whites, the influence of feminism upon political participation is less clearly traceable than among blacks. Since highly participant white women tend to be high in socioeconomic standing, and since high socioeconomic status women tend to be feminist, it is possible that interaction effects are contained within our coefficients. Additional research is needed, however, to assess such a possibility.

Based on these findings, path diagrams for each sample partition were made to provide a more visually interpretable outline of influences upon political participation. Direct, but not total, effects of the variables upon political participation are presented for white women and for minority women in Appendix B. Influences on the political participation of minority women are far more complex than those found for white women. Comparisons other than those discussed here may be made by the reader using the two figures in Appendix B together, in conjunction with the more extensive findings reported in Tables 7.6 and 7.7.

CONCLUSION

Clearly, the striking finding of this chapter is that the causal model argued in the research of how ideology affects behavior is, indeed, a powerful one. The model explained 55 percent of the variance in the political participation of white women and an astounding 72 percent of the variance in the political participation of minority women. The testing of such a model in the future with other ideologies and various subgroups of the population, both nationally and comparatively, seems to be a potentially strong heuristic tool for the study of the relationship between political ideology and political behavior.

Other noteworthy, but less powerful, findings are evident as well. First, we found that the relationship of feminism to the political behavior of women stayed basically constant over time, with direct relationships being significant but relatively weak. Minority women were found to be less participant than were white women, but to have a far stronger relationship between their feminism and their political participation than was true for white women. Glaring differences found in the role of socioeconomic factors in relation to feminism for white women and minority women led us to hypothesize that feminism was tapping a different sense of deprivation in each group—a sense of relative fraternal deprivation among white women, who compare themselves to high socioeconomic-status white males, and a sense of absolute deprivation among minority women, who feel they are doing poorly (both figuratively and literally) compared to everyone else.

Given these findings and the greater relationship between feminism and political participation among minority women, it was hypothesized that a low degree of political trust and a high sense of internal control, rather than a high sense of political efficacy, formed the vital combination of attitudes for stimulating political participation. Findings in the analysis of the causal model supported such a modification of alienation theory.

A path model predicting political behavior was offered that suggested that political ideology is formed as a product of socialization and life situation variables and that this occurs before the formation of specific political attitudes. It was argued that influences political attitudes, which, in turn, are the primary influences upon political behavior. The plausibility of these assumptions was supported strongly by the findings for both subsamples tested. Feminism turned out to be a significant predictor of the political participation of both white women and minority women, and was especially strong in its influence upon minority women.

The findings presented suggest that feminism, an ideology that expresses psychic discontent with the status quo, is most powerful in its practical political effects when adopted by persons who are also experiencing real material deprivation along with their psychological unrest. Feminism seems to have gained its most activist adherents among those who, objectively speaking, have gained the least materially from the reforms that feminism advocates.

Furthermore, the effects of feminism upon political participation are clearly strongest among that group of the electorate with perhaps the least political clout—that is, minority women. The comparatively small influence of feminism on white women's political participation, combined with the fact that feminism's influence upon the political participation of minority women is, chiefly, upon traditional forms of political behavior, suggests that hopes for feminism as an agent used by women for radical political change are far from realistic, at least for the near future. Overall changes in the mass political behavior of American women over the past four years simply do not support such hopes.

But in that statement may be cause for hope. As assessment of behavioral change over a period of only four years may be quite premature. Feminism does make a difference in the political behavior of American women—it is a moderate influence upon white women and a strong influence upon minority women. Yet it is both possible and plausible that not enough time has elapsed between the beginning and the end point of this study. Ideological influences upon political behavior appear to take time—perhaps substantially longer than four years. Thus, the very real difference that feminism can already be seen to have made in the political behavior of American women may be only the tip of the proverbial iceberg. If so, more time and research are needed to determine the eventual scope of the effects unearthed thus far. What is striking, of course, is that, even within a short period, feminism has had a real influence on the political behavior of American women. For minority women, that influence has been particularly strong.

NOTES

1. The regression coefficients reported in this and all tables dealing with political

participation have, as in Chapter 6, been computed in step-wise regression equations in which socioeconomic variables were entered prior to feminism, so that the spurious effects of Socioeconomic-Standard variables upon the relationship would not cloud the strength of the relationship represented by the regression coefficients.

2. For extensive discussion of causal modeling or path analysis see Blalock (1970, 1964).

3. See Appendix C for extended discussion of path analysis techniques and uses of causal modeling. The complete set of path equations and a discussion of decomposing effects of one variable upon another using multivariate regression techniques are also included there.

4. A strong counterargument to the latter assumption could, of course, be made. That is, one could argue that because of an individual's low sense of being able personally to control her environment she would then become feminist, and not vice versa. This seems less plausible, however, than the contention that feminism is likely to affect sense of internal control, since having such an effect is a direct objective within feminist ideology. Recent research (Riger 1977) tests the causal relation from sense of internal control to feminism and finds it not supported, which also adds strength to the flow diagram of this model. Realistically, it seems most plausible to assume a certain interaction or feedback loop between the two variables of feminism and internal control. Such a structure was not included in this model for two obvious reasons: (1) theoretical support for a causal flow from sense of internal control to feminism was far weaker than the reverse order posited; and (2) such a feedback loop would have greatly exaggerated the computational complexities of the model, since it would have required a nonrecursive model in which the basic recursive assumptions of zero-order correlations of paths would be violated.

5. For a full discussion of the mathematical assumptions and methods of the model refer to Knoche (1978), Chapter 7.

6. This supports Gelb's contention (1970) that blacks in the future will rely on political party politics as a vehicle for social change more heavily than they have in the past.

8

FEMINISM, IDEOLOGY, AND POLITICAL CHANGE

*V*isions of social change focus upon two conflicting sets of images. On the one hand, change appears ubiquitous, as scenes from Toffler's *Future Shock* (1970) suggest. Society is under constant stress from the speed of change in such old, traditional arenas as the nuclear family, marriage, life-styles, religion, occupational permanence, and secure communities. Contemporary times move quickly indeed and change seems to be a constant phenomenon of modern technological society.

On the other hand, change appears an impossible and utopian ideal, being painfully difficult for individuals, not to mention for tortoise-slow institutions such as the church, the government, and multinational corporations, which seem far more rigid than malleable. Institutional appearances, it is true, sometimes alter, but rarely does institutional substance. Institutions seem virtually impervious toward efforts to change exerted upon them by individuals or even by most groups. Both the scope and the complexity of large contemporary institutions give them the image of being unknowable and unalterable. There seems to be more wisdom than catchiness in the adage that "the more things change, the more they stay the same."

Yet each of these two apparently contradictory images of change is accurate in its own way. The first vision refers to the dynamic alterations in technology and social values that affect individuals' lives with seemingly ever-greater frequency and speed. The other vision deals with change that focuses upon institutions more than individuals, and is concerned with such things as redistribution of economic goods, social justice, and political power. Changes of this type occur slowly indeed.

Change occurs, or does not occur, simultaneously on both levels: on the individual and the institutional level, through both personal and political avenues. The two dimensions are interrelated and interactive. Yet this study has arbitrarily attempted to separate out and focus upon only processes of personal change. Now it is necessary to try to integrate, reassess, and analyze in a broader vein than has occurred thus far, so that the personal side of political change can once again be linked with the systemic or institutional side of change.

Two overriding foci directed this study. One was the role that social movements play in the process of political change. The other was the role of political ideology as an influence upon political behavior. The specific vehicle for studying these two broad questions was the contemporary feminist movement. Specifically, four major research questions were addressed in an attempt to deepen our knowledge of the way social movements and political ideology relate to processes of change in political behavior. (1) To what extent is feminism a political ideology? (2) How do feminist ideology and its various political attitudinal and behavioral relationships differ among major social groups—that is, men and women, whites and nonwhites? (3) To what extent does feminism influence political attitudes? (4) How does feminism affect the political behavior of American women?

Throughout the discussion, however, several other, loosely related questions have appeared, all concerned with the theme of social change. The role of political participation as important within the process of political change has largely been assumed and needs explicit treatment. The role of ideology as a mediator between personal and systemic dimensions of political change has been intermingled with other discussion in the analysis. Feminism has provided the ideological framework for the total analysis and, yet, in a more inclusive sense, the potential impact of feminism upon the political system has not been focused upon directly. A social movement— the feminist movement or any other—does act as both a symptom and a cause of social change. The empirical analysis of the study reflected assumptions that feminism was an independent variable, an effector. Feminism also needs to be considered as a dependent variable, as the product of other aspects of social change. A look at these grander themes should present implications of this study for wider questions of political theory than those yet addressed.

But first we need to refresh our memory on the major conclusions substantiated by these data, making explicit various connections between them and the other themes just mentioned above. Four major findings stand out. Crucially, feminism is making a difference politically. Feminism was found, clearly, to influence the way women relate to the political system. Secondly, feminism was found to be a political ideology. Both theoretically and empirically, feminism showed itself to be ideological and to impinge uniquely upon American women. Thirdly, feminism was seen not to be affecting all women in the same way. White and minority women related to and were affected by feminism in different ways. Lastly, and perhaps most importantly, the causal model tested here proved to be a powerful heuristic tool for further political research on the nature and influences of mass belief systems.

MAJOR FINDINGS OF THE STUDY

Feminism Makes a Difference Politically

Feminism makes a difference for how women relate to the political system. This finding above all else stands out from this study. Feminism affects the political attitudes of women and, more importantly, this author believes, their political behavior. Moreover, *in each instance studied*, effects of feminism upon the political attitudes and political behavior of white women were overshadowed by the substantially stronger effects of feminism upon minority women.

Much has been written over the past decade concerning the real and imagined effects of feminism upon American women, the fabric of family life, sexual mores, and multitudinous other aspects of modern culture. Little, however, has been documented in any respectable way about the effects of feminism upon the political attitudes and behavior of American women. As this study showed, such effects are both real and substantive.

Feminism Is a Political Ideology

This study argued that feminism has been increasingly reflecting and expressing a basic political ideology that embodies descriptions of social reality, value statements, and programmatic suggestions for social change. The content of this ideology revolves around the idea that appropriate roles for women involve equality with men, that the dominant American ideology is sexist, and that discrimination, exploitation, and oppression of women are characteristic of U.S. society. Contemporary feminist ideology makes strong normative statements, arguing for equality in many forms— economic, political, and psychological—and in many societal sectors— including the marketplace, the home, the House, the church, and the Senate. Feminism has notions of how women ought to be treated in these different areas and how, for example, gender roles ought to be modified or eliminated within them. To promote these values and help bring about these goals, feminist ideology takes strategic and tactical stands advocating freedom of choice through abortion rights, passage of the Equal Rights

Amendment, affirmative action policies, antidiscrimination laws for lesbians and male homosexuals, credit law equalization, protection for displaced homemakers and battered wives, and so on. Feminist ideology describes reality, evaluates it, and maps roads society needs to follow to reach a feminist destination.

Empirically, as well as conceptually, feminism was found to be structured ideologically. When the sample was partitioned by ability groups, feminism turned out to be centered around a notion of egalitarian roles, to be tightly structured, and to be closely related to liberal-conservative ideology among higher-ability groups of both sexes. Feminism gave clear evidence of possessing the characteristics of centrality and constraint, which according to Converse are essential to political ideology.

In short, feminism is a political ideology—both in terms of item structure and in terms of the nature of its content. In fact, feminism possesses ideological traits to a greater extent than does the liberal-conservative ideology studied by Converse (1964). While certain earlier scholars have been dubious about the ideological nature of feminism, empirical analysis of ideological structure in this study showed that feminism is indeed ideological.

Feminism among Women Is Not Equal to Feminism among Men

Not only has feminism proven to be a political ideology, but it has proven to be a political ideology that impinges uniquely upon women. Feminism among women is more tightly structured than feminism among men. Feminism among women is closely linked to certain psychological constructs. This is not true for men. Values are central to the content of feminism for women, while for men feminism is primarily a descriptive belief set. Feminism is more extremely or intensely held for women than for men. Further, feminism is strongly related to certain key life situations, such as marital status and age, only for women. The evidence is clear and strong. Feminism is a central and important belief set for women, a more peripheral one for men.

Feminism among White Women Is Not Equal to Feminism among Minority Women

Perhaps the most outstanding and the least expected finding of this study was that minority women respond quite differently to feminism than do white women. From the earliest stages of the data analysis, this was evident. While white women and men, and even black men, were becoming more feminist between 1972 and 1976, support for feminism among minority women dropped startlingly.

No such finding was forecast or documented from other research. A new, significant phenomenon was evident. When it came to beliefs about organizing women, about abortion, and about the women's movement, minority women were, in 1976, reversing the views they held in 1972. Where previously minority women were the most feminist group surveyed, by 1976 they had become the least feminist, a surprising occurrence by any measure.

But changes in support for feminism because of race were only the beginning of of race-related findings unearthed in these data. Changes in support for feminism were indicators, flags, of more deeply seated impacts of feminism upon minority women. Not only were minority women responding differently to feminism by supporting some components of feminist ideology, such as ideas of equality and discrimination, more strongly than whites, and opposing other items more strongly, but they were also responding more strongly to feminism than were white women with reference to their political attitudes and political behavior.

Influences of feminism upon political attitudes and political behavior were strikingly stronger for minority women than for white women in case after case. Feminism explained more about the ultimate political behavior of minority women than did any variable tested, with the exception of personal political attitudes. Furthermore, personal political attitudes among minority women were themselves more influenced by feminism than by any other variable: minority women were the most extreme in their stand on feminist items, and more influenced by feminism than were white women in every measure tested.

THE CAUSAL MODEL

Prediction in social science is an extremely difficult task, and theoretical modeling is often avoided. The causal model presented and tested here of how ideology influences political behavior generated sufficient predictive power that it merits special attention at this point. Although the predictive power of the model was lowest for white women, explaining 55 percent of the total variance in their political participation, the achieved prediction was still quite respectable. For minority women, the power of the model rose to explain an impressive 72 percent of the total variance in political participation. Both figures are substantial indeed.

Strong support has been found with these data for the belief that ideas influence behavior, as well as for the argument that the influence of ideology upon political behavior follows the direction or paths illustrated within the causal model offered in Chapter 7. Particular demographic and sociological factors seem to exert the earliest influences upon later political behavior, as this model and practitioners and theoreticians from Freud to Lane have argued. Psychological and ideological belief sets appear to form next, chronologically, and to be primary influences upon the personal and system-focused political attitudes that the individual holds. Each of these prior variables directly, and indirectly through various intervening variables, influenced individual political behavior.

THEORETICAL ISSUES

The findings of these data have raised some provocative theoretical issues that merit a bit more attention. For instance, we have seen that ideology is both interpreted and applied differently for different groups of people, yet have not explored what that may mean for the study of ideology. The finding that political attitudes do function as intervening variables in the relationship between ideology and political behavior warrants some amplification. Our understanding of how race mediates the role feminism plays in political participation has also been increased. Generally speaking, the way in which ideas influence behavior has been clarified by the study of feminist ideology. Let us explore this a bit.

Ideological Structure and Social Groups

First, that feminist ideology differs in terms of content, extremism, structure, and salience for different groups in society says some clear things for the study of ideologies other than feminism. For one thing, ideological content—ideas—can be, and in this case was, stressed differently by different groups. Even given almost exactly comparable agreement score totals on a series of ideology-related items, different people respond and relate to the same items differently. To the extent that these differences simply reflect personal idiosyncratic responses, error and score differences will be randomly distributed overall. Statistical inferences will, thus, not be significantly affected. Where such differences cluster by social groups, however, this will not be the case. Substantive results of analysis will differ. Care needs to be taken, therefore, in conducting research, to analyze groups with differing theoretical links to the ideology under investigation in ways that allow results to be carefully compared for various groups.

Clear group differences existed in these data on several fronts. Content differences, for instance, were clear, and content analysis of ideology has generally been undertreated, at best, and ignored, at worst, in studies of political ideology. The inference from this research is that some content considerations are both necessary and helpful in any full analysis of ideology.

In addition, relationships between the ideology of feminism and psychological variables varied by group. Links among women were strong and those among men almost nonexistent. This research says, clearly, that both the cognitive and the psychological dimensions have something important to say about the significance or salience of ideology for the individual. Which content items are ranked most and least highly and how the total ideological structure relates to the psychological perceptions of the individual both affect the importance and the impact of the ideology upon any particular person.

Ideology is not monolithic—either in its structure or in the influence it has upon different social groups. For research to treat ideology as though it were a monolith represents a serious impediment to the expansion of the knowledge and theory available for the study of political belief systems.

Feminism and Political Attitudes

Political attitudes were viewed in this study as intervening variables between ideology and political behavior. Thus, it is assumed, as the social experiences of the individual unfold and impinge upon the person, political attitudes are substantially influenced by feminist ideology; they also have a major influence upon the actual political behavior that the individual engages in.

The findings of this study provided support for that assumption in several important ways. First, as support for feminism strengthened over time, so did the relationship between feminism and political attitudes. Feminism turned out to enhance most personal political attitudes—such as sense of citizen duty, political interest, whether participation in protest activities was deemed acceptable, and the like—but to be related to a low sense of political efficacy. Simply put, feminists in 1976 obviously believed themselves to be less politically effective than they had in 1972. Feminism for minority women was related to these attitudes even more strongly than was true for white women. With reference to system-related political attitudes, white and minority women responded comparably—but, again, effects of feminism were strongest among minority women. For both groups, political trust was lower for feminists in 1976 than in 1972, but perceptions of government attentiveness were higher. Men running the system were generally distrusted, while belief was maintained in the capacity of the system itself to respond to people's demands and needs. Of course, it is unclear whether the explanation for these findings was also a product of definite ambivalence on the part of women in their understanding of how the system was helping or hindering efforts toward change in women's rights and roles. What was clear was that, while feminism among both white and minority women was linked with signs of political alienation, these associations were far stronger among minority women than among white women.

When political attitudes were considered as an intervening variable between feminism and political behavior, then, strong support was found for the view that feminism does influence political attitudes. Yet even stronger support was found for the contention that political attitudes influence behavior. Political attitudes dominated as predictors of political participation for both groups of women, explaining nearly half the variance in total participation scores for the entire sample. Political attitudes of individuals form and change partially as a result of the influence of ideology. Political attitudes themselves also have a major influence upon how individuals behave politically. Attitudes do act as intervening variables in the relationship between ideology and political participation.

Feminism and Political Behavior

More than any other influence considered in the study, race resulted in profound differences in the effects of feminism upon political behavior. Feminism turned out to be significantly related to all forms of conventional political participation for minority women in 1976, and more strongly related to each of the six composite participation indices for these women than for white women. While feminism's direct effects upon political behavior were generally weak, the indirect effects of feminism upon political behavior through political attitudes were moderately strong. One of the social influences that effect attitude change and lead to behavior was clearly feminist ideology—for both white and minority women.

The striking finding, of course, was the central role feminism played as an influence upon the political behavior of minority women. Only personal political attitudes were more strongly predictive of the political participation of minority women than feminism. But the ways (paths) by which feminism influenced participation, as well as the strength (coefficients) of such influence, differed considerably depending upon race. For both groups, feminism's influence upon personal political attitudes was most central. For minority women, however, this was only one of four ways in which feminism influenced participation (the others being through sense of internal control, sense of government responsiveness, and political trust), whereas for white women the effect of feminism upon political behavior appeared to occur only through personal political attitudes.

Ideology, Political Attitudes And Political Behavior

What has occurred with feminism, political attitudes, and political behavior reveals intriguing possibilities for the relationships among ideology, political attitudes, and political behavior. For one, assumptions of political theory that ideas do influence action have received strong support in this research. Both unified political belief systems and specific political attitudes had such an impact. Most crucially, attitudes do mediate between political belief systems and specific kinds of political behavior.

Ideologies that speak directly to conceptions of justice and inequality, as feminism does, may influence political behavior in the following manner. As people learn—formally or experientially—that they are, supposedly, free and equal persons in the eyes of the democratic system, they come to expect that, indeed, they *ought* to be free, equal, and justly treated. The ideology they learn and believe describes reality in such a way that normative evaluations and goals are established by the individual. When this kind of belief set is combined with attitudes of dissatisfaction (low political trust, low evaluation of government, and so on) coupled with a sense of personal competence (internal control), individuals may soon come to believe both that they *can* act politically in ways that would improve their life situation and that they *ought* to take such action. When such attitudinal combinations occur, greater political participation is likely.

Causal arrows were assumed to run in one direction only in the theoretical model of political behavior tested here. Yet evidence indicates another possibility. Because low political efficacy was associated with feminism for both white and minority women, it is plausible that actual participation is not usually effective for women and that unsuccessful efforts at participation instill or reinforce a low sense of political efficacy in believers of a major reform-oriented ideology like feminism. Such unsuccessful efforts, in turn, could reinforce the perceived accuracy of the descriptions of reality that the dissident ideology holds up. Causal arrows well may run in both directions between ideology and participation in some cases, and should be so tested in other research.

Disparities between preaching and practice within a political system, between an ideology and the existing status quo, may serve as one measure of the likelihood of little success for the efforts of believers of the alternative ideology. Hence, such disparities may act as a measure, too, of the likelihood of reciprocal causality between an ideology and political behavior.

Various explanations have been offered in the literature for the low substantiation found thus far (discussed at some length earlier) of the Gamson hypothesis that the attitudinal combination of a low level of trust and a high sense of efficacy is the one most likely to result in greater political participation. Several other considerations in that theory are illustrated here from this study's findings.

First, for those persons experiencing absolute deprivation—that is, poverty—the likelihood that a low level of political trust will be associated with political participation of even a traditional sort seems to be greater than among higher socioeconomic status people. Secondly, higher socioeconomic-status persons—for the purposes of this research, white women—are more likely to have a higher sense of political efficacy and to have that sense of political efficacy related to their political participation than are lower-income persons. But *both* groups are likely to have a high sense of internal control related to participation.

The conjecture, then, that basically unconventional types of participation will be associated with a low level of political trust and that primarily conventional participation will be associated with a low level of political trust and that primarily conventional participation will be associated with a high sense of political efficacy (Seligson 1977) was not supported. Clear differences in the association between these political attitudes and political participation did not occur in these data. Social-group factors such as race and sex simply appeared more important in explaining the relationships between attitudes and behavior than did participation type alone. Sense of political efficacy, largely a function of socioeconomic status, seemed less important as a predictor than did sense of internal control, especially when socioeconomic standing was low. What seems likely to determine which attitudinal variables more affect political participation is the salience of each of these variables for the life situation of the individual—and that seems largely to be a function of life experience within one's social group, as well as a function of the interpretation that feminist or other ideology gives to that experience.[1]

SOCIAL CHANGE

Change *is* a constant—perhaps not major or revolutionary change, but clearly incremental and personal change. The big questions do not revolve around such issues as "Can change occur?" and "Will change occur?" We all know the answer to both these questions to be a definite yes. The key topics dealing with change instead center around the content, direction, scope, and rate of change. These are the obvious concerns of social movements and of ideologices. What will change and what will remain unaltered? Will the change be an improvement or a regression? How extensive will change be? How quickly will it come?

Basic change—major changes in the distribution of social rewards and benefits, deep value changes—involve a dual process. Basic changes require personal change in the values, attitudes, and behavior of large numbers of people, and they also require change on the part of the social and political system. Both are necessary. Neither alone is sufficient.

Yet this study, quite obviously, has focused on only one side of the social change question: how and to what extent individuals are changing. It has also, more specifically, focused on how contemporary feminism is affecting personal political attitude and behavior change in the electorate. It would be remiss to leave the discussion so one-sided.

Political Participation and Social Change

While acknowledging that system response is a necessary condition for lasting social change, this study, ultimately, has focused upon individual behavior change. Why?

The root assumption should be clear. The bias of the study is that participation matters, that it makes a difference. Such an assumption requires justification.

In one sense, such a statement immediately appears false. Writing these words, as I am, on a day when the Equal Rights Amendment was defeated for the second consecutive time in the Illinois legislature this session and knowing, as I do, personally, scores of women who have contributed great personal effort to try to prevent this defeat, it is not easy to claim that participation makes a difference. But I do claim that.

However, I also do not claim that political participation *necessarily* makes a difference. Claims and requests addressed to the political system may be ignored, symbolically sidetracked, or superficially flustered and blustered over. They also may never even be attended to in the slightest. Participation does not necessarily lead to political redress or even to a political hearing. Participation may not be sufficient, but in many situations it is necessary.

Political theorists, of course, also pose the notion that a participatory society is one of the requirements of the ideal political system. For them, participation has certain values as an end in itself. Contemporary political theory generally recognizes that both stability and change in democratic systems are a function of the social system they help organize. Much of this theory, especially that large portion dealing with social pluralism, focuses more upon stability as a goal of political systems than upon change within that system. Such an emphasis tends to lead to instituional forms of analysis rather than to analyses dealing with processes. The focus of this particular work has been, intrinsically, upon process—specifically, upon processes of change that relate to feminism and political ideology.

But this study, after all, focused upon the current women's movement and feminist political ideology. To what extent does any of this theoretical discussion apply there? Does feminism appear to be affecting social change in any basic ways?

Several observations stand out. The rise in agreement with feminist values and perceptions of reality from 1972 to 1976 gives evidence that an alternative vision of the ideal society—a vision that does involve major redistribution of power, goods, and status—has become more accepted. Thus, the influence of a relatively small group's ideology (that is, the ideology of current women's movement leaders) has had a significant impact upon mass ideology. If these feminist perceptions of an egalitarian social ideal remain starkly juxtaposed with an inegalitarian reality, it seems plausible to argue that the already clear attitudinal and behavioral linkages with feminist ideology will become stronger. Whether the political attitudinal and behavioral changes that might result will, in any way, evoke a clear and meaningful response on the part of the political system, however, cannot be assessed from this study.

Given the clear connections for white women between socioeconomic factors and feminism, some further conjectures are in order. Widely held middle- and upper-middle-class values tend to be supported by the dominant political ideology and reward structure of U.S. society (Huber and Form 1973; Best and Connolly 1975). Middle-class values tend to predominate. Thus, feminist support among this group in 1976 may portend feminist support among lower socioeconomic groups in later years. Feminism well may be the new and socially accepted value set for younger Americans, as the strong associations between feminism and youth tend to indicate.

To whatever extent support for feminist values grows, we have seen strong support in this study for the expectation that important political norms are changing for women. Perceptions of equality and inequality are clearly being altered. Women want and value economic equality to an extent not true before. Support for new, more androgynous sex roles is growing, with women believing in the value of organizing and in the desirability of women having equal roles to men in the political arena as well. If ideology affects behavior through attitude change (an idea this study supports), a certain time lag between acceptance of feminist ideology and the appearance of political attitude change and then political behavior change would seem likely. If this is the case, these data may be revealing only the tip of the iceberg in terms of long-range political behavior change that has been influenced by present-day feminist ideology.

How such personal behavior change might express itself in terms of type of behavior, however, we can only guess. Among white women, political behavior directly traceable to feminism is slight. Among minority women, such behavioral links are far stronger but are found primarily with traditional political behavior. If the traditional behavior now associated with minority feminism continues, however, and benefits to these women do not rise, we may well see a marked increase in the relationship between feminism and nonconventional forms of political behavior in this group in the future. The higher sense of both political trust and political efficacy found among white women, on the other hand, would suggest that this group might first attempt more traditional political activity as the relationship between feminism and political behavior strengthens. White women seem less clearly on the verge of widespread participation in nontraditional political behavior than minority women appear to be.

The high and rising support for feminist ideas among white men, black men, and white women provides hope for a wide base of legitimacy for response to feminist demands. The extent to which the system does respond to these demands may itself be the most influential determinant of the kinds of effects on political behavior that feminist ideology will have in the future. But just as no social movement can be expected to appeal evenly to all segments of society, neither can it be expected to influence or have an impact upon all social groups evenly. The clear differences thus far in the impact of feminism upon white women and minority women strongly suggest that future differences in the influence of feminism will exist between major social groups as well.

One other thing is certain. The weak relationship found between feminism and nonconventional political behavior for both black women and white women implies a strong core of support for traditional, moderate, gradual reform efforts toward social change. Radical support of feminism and a tendency toward radical action (as measured by extreme agreement scores) are both absent from these data. That fact, more than anything else, may predict the scope and type of system response that feminism will evoke.

This study, however, has made some understandings about feminism and social change in today's United States vividly clear. Feminism is a political ideology, and one to which a majority of Americans give general support. Feminism for men, however, is not the same as feminism for women. For women, feminism is a far more central and personally significant set of issues than is true for men. Similarly, feminism for minority women is both supported differently and responded to more strongly with respect to political attitudes and behavior than is true for white women. The overall finding of the study for either minority or white women in the United States is clear: *feminism is making a difference in how women relate to the U.S. political system.* This present second wave of U.S. feminism is altering the relation of women to the body politic. Personal political changes are occurring in American women as a result of contemporary feminism.

What does all this imply for the future impact of feminism upon U.S. politics? My presumption (as well as my hope) based on these findings is that feminism's influence has only begun to be felt. If agreement with feminist notions continues to expand as it did in the period between 1972 and 1976 (and we have no reason to suppose that it will not), then several things are likely to occur. For one, women are likely to become increasingly aware of and angry over sex-based inequities in this social system and more adamant for change. In addition, men are likely to come to see women's demands as more and more valid, so that some resistance to feminist-based change should lessen. Furthermore, as women's roles continue to change, they are likely to develop the skills and attitudes that will make them both more politically effective and more likely to seek political activity. Now we are seeing sharply rising participation by women at local political levels. It is likely that this trend will continue and will serve as a training ground for greater female activism on the state and national level.

Attitudinal change preceeds behavioral change. Attitudinal change is already occurring, and time should translate this change into widespread behavioral changes for women as well. I would expect that greater political activism by women is going to evidence itself in greater local involvement, interest-group activity, and political party leadership. All of these trends are likely to contribute to an overall rise in women's political activism at all levels.

I doubt, however, that these trends will be constant for minority women. The data suggest high levels of political alienation among these women. That is likely to mean that their activism will be less directly expressed in electoral politics and more evidently centered around specific causes, local community needs, and the like. Until minority women see the system serving them more directly and equitably, they are not likely to provide it with widespread support. They are, however, increasingly, likely to compaign stridently for issues that affect them directly. In the long run, this, too, will propel minority women also into positions of political leadership, but not at the pace with which this occurs among white women.

Precisely how much change is occurring and will occur in how the American political system responds to women and the demands feminism makes of the system in this era still remains an open, empirical question. One thing is clear: change in women and in their role perceptions, their attitudes, and the way they relate to the political system is occurring. Forces resistant to such changes—whether blatantly sexist or just frustratingly obstinate—will themselves be the objects of change over time. Social institutions, gender roles, individuals' attitudes, and political system policies are not immutable. Whether aberrant or noble in spirit, societies do not maintain themselves in a single, rigid set of social structures over indefinite periods of time. Some change is constant. The rate at which that change speeds up or slows down will vary with the rate of aggregate personal change and system response. The dynamics of interaction between the two aspects of change determine the speed, extent, and direction of change. If either dimension moves at a rate that far exceeds the other, discontent will accelerate rapidly—either on the part of persons frustrated with the caterpillar crawl of the system's response or on the part of the system's leaders alarmed over the seemingly percipitous demands of the masses. Political and social change can come either at the rate of the caterpillar's crawl or the speed of its metamorphosis into a butterfly.

Resistance to the kind and rate of change urged by feminism and other social movement ideologies in recent years has often been intense. Whether that resistance will succeed in slowing down the process of change to the seemingly infinitely slow rate of the caterpillar's progress along a 12-foot branch, or whether the basically revolutionary changes requested of the system will appear as suddenly as do fields of monarch butterflies in late summer, only time and further study will tell.

But even the short life span of caterpillars, like that of feminists, is marked by efforts of movement and change. How that change is being expressed in personal political attitudes and behavior and what that change might portend for the political metamorphosis of American women have been the objects of this study.

NOTE

1. It is especially important here to recognize that such contaminants as social class, education, income, and the like were first accomodated in estimating the regression coefficients generated in this study, and that the coefficients presented throughout represent the effects of feminism upon the various variables after such contamination has been removed.

APPENDIX A:
THE CODING OF
FEMINISM ITEMS

In devising the feminism index, two controls were needed: (1) a guarantee that agreement existed about which item responses were feminist ones, so that such a crucial matter was not a purely arbitrary decision made by the researcher alone; and (2) agreement as to the kind of ideological content tapped by each item, so that, too, would not be a decision made personally and arbitrarily on the part of the researcher.

To accommodate both these needs, a panel of 24 judges was enlisted to make each of these decisions. The panel consisted of 21 advanced graduate students in political science and 3 political science faculty members. Each judge read and coded the 11 feminist items independently from other judges. Decision rules used in categorizing items were explained in Chapter 4.

Each judge was asked to do two things: (1) select from all possible responses to each item the response that she or he considered the most feminist; and (2) place each item (as contrasted to responses to the item) in one of the following categories: a description of social reality, a value statement, or a prescription for social change. That is, each judge was asked to decide whether the survey respondent was being asked to agree or disagree with a descriptive statement, a value statement, or a social change program when responding to that item. With the exception of the three faculty members, each of whom was able to ask individual questions of the researcher concerning the instructions, other judges were able to ask oral questions or request clarifications of directions. All judges were given the following form to complete.

Dear
I find in coding my dissertation data I need the benefit of an impartial "panel of judges". Would you please lend me the benefit of your wisdom and about 15 minutes of your time? It really would help me; I'd appreciate it very much.

Please read through the set of eleven items twice and do the following two things. 1) First, read each item and then indicate which of the possible responses strikes you as the "most feminist". Place the letter or number of this response in the blank at the left of the item. 2) On the second reading decide whether each item as a whole could best be categorized as a) a description of social reality, b) a value statement (a should/shouldn't, good/bad evaluation), or c) a prescription for social change (i.e., what is needed to bring about some desired state). Fill in the blank on the right of each item with the following indication of your best judgment as to content categorization of the item: DSR for a description of social reality, VS for value statement, or SC for prescription of social change.

Please complete the form at your earliest convenience and return to my mailbox. Many thanks.

Claire

Most Feminist Response	Item	Content Category
_____	1) What is your opinion of the amount of influence women have as a group? Do you think women as a group have a) too much influence, b) not enough influence, or c) just about the right amount of influence?	_____
_____	2) Some people feel that women should have an equal role with men in running business, industry, and government. Others feel that women's place is in the home. Where would you place yourself on this scale? 1) Women's place is in the home?, 7) Women and men should have an equal role?, or somewhere between 1) and 7)?	_____
_____	3) There has been some discussion of abortion in recent years. Which one of the opinions presented here best agrees with your view? a) Abortion should never be permitted. b) Abortions should be permitted only if the life and health of the woman is in danger, c) Abortion should be permitted if, due to personal reasons, the woman would have difficulty in caring for the child. d) Abortion should never be forbidden, since one should not require a woman to have a child she doesn't want.	_____
	4) Sometimes a company has to lay off parts of its labor force.	

a) Some people think that the first workers to be laid off should be women whose husbands have jobs. b) Others think that male and female employees should be treated the same. Which of these opinions do you agree with?

5) Which of these two statements do you agree with? a) Many qualified women can't get good jobs; men with the same skills have much less trouble. Or. b) In general, men are more qualified than women for jobs that have great responsibility.

6) Which of these two statements do you most agree with? a) Women can best overcome discrimination by pursuing their individual career goals in as feminine a way as possible. Or. b) It is not enough for a woman to be successful herself; women must work together to change laws and customs that are unfair to all women.

7) Which of these two statements do you most agree with? a) It's more natural for men to have the top responsible jobs in a country. Or. b) Sex discrimination keeps women from the top jobs.

8) Which of these two statements do you most agree with? a) The best way to handle problems of discrimination is for each woman to make sure she gets the best training possible for what she wants to do. Or. b) Only if women organize and work together can anything really be done about discrimination.

9) Which of these two statements do you most agree with? a) By nature women are happiest when they are making a home and caring

for children. Or. b) Our society, not nature, teaches women to prefer homemaking to work outside the home.

10) Which of these two statements do you most agree with? a) Men have more of the top jobs because they are born with more drive to be ambitious and successful than women. Or. b) Men have more of the top jobs because our society discriminates against women.

11) On a "feeling thermometer" ranging from 0 degrees to 100 degrees (actually 97 degrees), how warm would you say you feel toward the women's liberation movement? (Respondents were instructed that ratings between 51 and 100 degrees meant they felt warm and favorable towards the women's liberation movement; ratings of 0 to 49 meant they did not feel favorably toward the movement; and a rating of 50 meant they felt neutral or had no feelings about the movement.)

APPENDIX B:
CAUSAL ANALYSIS
CHARTS

FIGURE B. 1: Direct Effects upon Political Participation of White Women, 1976.

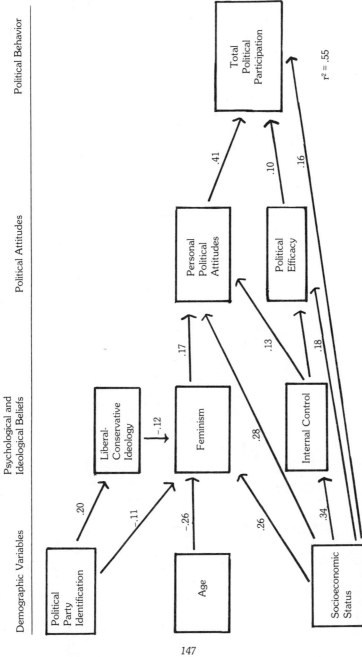

Note: N = 501. Entries are betas. Only paths greater than .10 are entered.
Source: Compiled by the author.

147

FIGURE B. 2: Direct Effects upon the Political Participation of Minority Women, 1976

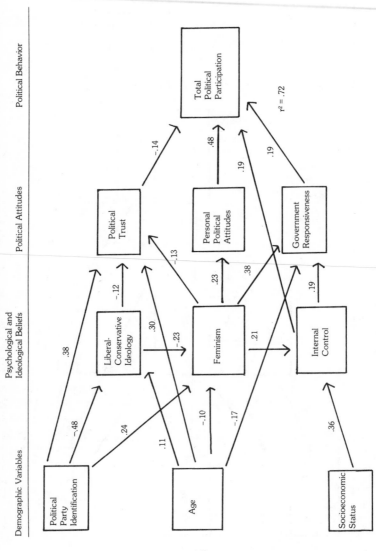

| Demographic Variables | Psychological and Ideological Beliefs | Political Attitudes | Political Behavior |

Note: N = 85. All entries are betas. Only paths greater than .10 are entered.
Source: Compiled by the author.

148

APPENDIX C:
CAUSAL MODELING
AND PATH ANALYSIS

Although causal modeling has become an increasingly used analytic and heuristic tool in the social sciences generally in recent years, its use within political science remains both infrequent and frequently misunderstood. The purpose of this appendix is to provide a clear and simple description of this form of analysis in hope that its appeal and understanding will be enhanced.

CAUSAL ANALYSIS AND THEORIZING

First, a word about causal analysis in the most general sense is in order. While path analysis based on a causal model may be a powerful explanatory and predictive tool for actual data analysis, certain situations and conditions often make its use either impossible or incorrect. Some of these conditions will be discussed below. Even in such situations, however, causal theorizing may be highly helpful without actual path analysis. Thinking about a problem theoretically and developing causal hypotheses that may illustrate the conceived relationships by the use of an arrow diagram can be extremely useful in clarifying the research question and generating additional insights about it (see Van Meter and Asher 1973.)

The functional significance of causal diagrams is at least threefold. For one, they specify relationships between independent variables and the ultimate dependent variable. In addition, relationships among prior variables are made explicit and graphically conceptualized. Lastly, each linkage depicted in the diagram implicitly represents another hypothesis to be tested, through its generating of an estimate of the relationship's magnitude. Even though actual estimates may not be possible, for a variety of reasons, the important point is that the causal thinking illustrated in the diagram is more likely to increase understanding of the phenomena under study than is isolated correlation of independent and dependent variables without such explicitly integrated thought.

THE NOTION OF CAUSALITY

Causal modeling never allows one to determine the direction of causality in a model. This fact can not be given too much stress. The direction of causality *must* be established theoretically prior to analysis. Techniques of causal modeling also do not allow one to prove that a causal relationship exists. Such techniques can lend strong support to causal hypotheses, but they do not offer definitive proof of their validity.

Clearly, however, path analysis offers stronger support to inferences of causality than do of simple multiple regression techniques or other statistical devices common in political science. To infer the existence of a causal relationship between two variables, X and Y, three conditions must be met (Selltiz et al. 1959). First, there must be concomitant variation or covariation between the two variables. Second, a temporal relationship ought to exist such that the existence of one variable precedes the existence of the other. This, of course, may be argued theoretically or established objectively. But third, and most problematic, other possible causal factors or relationships ought to be eliminated if they conceivably could produce the observed relationship between variables X and Y. This last condition, put in other words, asserts that if a causal relationship does indeed exist between X and Y, the covariation found between these two variables must not vanish when the effects of other potentially confounding variables are removed. Since the universe of such confounding variables theoretically includes all variables that are causally prior to both X and Y, the possible universe of such variables is infinite—hence, the impossibility of ever eliminating totally spuriousness as a possibility in a hypothesized relationship (for example, owning a blue nine-week-old puppy may indeed be the true cause for low political trust among minority women, as it remains an untested hypothesis).

This latter condition clearly requires that we rule out all other possible causal factors from a potentially infinite universe of factors (Asher 1976). How can this be done? Clearly, no statistical test or coefficient can tell a researcher that the choice of causality that has been made is the correct one. All one can do is try to identify all theoretically logical confounding variables and formally include them in the model being tested. Yet, at some point closure must be established and a finite set of variables examined. Those variables must be decided upon for of theoretical reasons alone. As Blalock argues (1964, p. 26):

> No matter how elaborate the design, certain simplifying assumptions must always be made. In particular, we must at some point assume that the effects of confounding factors are negligible. Randomization helps to rule out some of such variables, but the plausibility of this particular kind of simplifying assumption is always a question of degree.

Mathematically, other possible influencing variables are allowed for by introducing error terms into the analysis. The assumption, of course, is that outside effects are sufficiently random that they exert no systematic effects upon the relationship between any two designated variables, X and Y, within the model.

RECURSIVE PATH ANALYSIS

Essentially, path analysis estimates the magnitude of linkages among variables. Then, using these estimates of magnitude, path analysis provides a means of calculating information about underlying causal processes. One of the main advantages of path analysis over other statistical techniques commonly employed in the social sciences is that it enables one to measure both direct and indirect effects of one variable upon another. In this way, it enables the analyst to examine causal processes that underlie specified and observed relationships and to compare the relative importance of various variables, knowing their total influence upon the dependent variable under study.

Path coefficients may be obtained in several ways, all of which employ ordinary least squares regression techniques. Before discussing and illustrating the application of such techniques to path analysis, however, it is important to review the basic assumptions implicit in such a form of analysis. These assumptions, of course, are parametric since path analysis is a correlation (regression) technique. Briefly stated, these assumptions are as follows:

1. Change in one variable always occurs as a linear function of changes in others (that is, interaction terms, polynomials, and transformation of variables that are often included in linear regression often cannot be accommodated with path models).

2. The path model (the equation system) must be recursive; that is, the model may not imply any feedback loops or reciprocal linkages. (Mathematically, this would be expressed such that if in a recursive system $p_{ij} \neq 0$, then $p_{ji} = 0$.)

3. Generally, the causal ordering among variables must be assumed theoretically. The directionality of the arrows is not a testable proposition.

4. Assumptions about correlations of distrubance (error) terms with each other and with the variables in the model must be made. Typical assumptions are that correlations of error terms equal zero. The assumption of lack of correlation is residuals basically is equivalent to asserting that there is no variable impinging upon any two measured variables within the system such that it directly influences two or more of the measured variables.

5. In addition, the normal assumptions of multiple linear regression hold:

    a. Empirical measurements are on an interval or "near interval" scale.
    b. For each structural equation, the disturbance term is uncorrelated with the independent variables in the equation.
    c. Disturbance terms are homoscadactic (having equal variances).
    d. Measurement of empirical data has high reliability and validity.

A causal model that is linear and recursive is a path model. Such a model can be described by a set of mathematical equations of the form:

$$x_i = \sum_{j=1}^{n} p_{ij} x_j + \text{(a disturbance term)},$$

where (1) x_i references the various endogenous variables in the model, (2) the x_js are exogenous and endogenous variables in the model that are causally prior to the given x_i, (3) all the Xs are understood to be in standardized form, and (4) path coefficients are directional such that p_{ij} is read as the "path to i from j." (In other words x_i is always a dependent variable—although not necessarily the ultimate dependent variable—and x_j is the independent variable.) An equation of this form needs to be made for every simple and every compound path (represented by arrows) in the model. Unfortunately, this procedure is quite tedious (see Goldberger 1970).

Another simpler and equally accurate method for computing paths based on all the same mathematical assumptions and theorems exists using Wright's (1934) rules. This procedure allows the analyst simply to read the simple and the compound paths directly from the arrow diagram itself. Applying this technique, however, requires that the analyst specify the following rules:

1. Any correlation between two variables can be decomposed into a sum of simple and compound paths.
2. A compound path is equal to the product of the simple paths comprising it.
3. No path may pass through the same variable more than once.
4. No path may go backward on (against the direction of) an arrow after the path has gone forward on a different arrow,
5. No path may pass through a double-headed curved arrow (representing an unanalyzed correlation between exogenous variables) more than once in any single path.

To summarize, recursive path analysis techniques tell us all that the Simon-Blalock technique tells us plus substantially more, and it does so with no additional cost in assumption requirements. Path analysis is superior to ordinary least squares regression analysis because it allows the analyst to move beyond estimating direct effects, the basic output of regression analysis. Path analysis allows both direct and indirect effects of one variable upon another to be examined. Thus, it makes possible an examination of the causal processes that underly observed relationships and an estimation of the relative importance of various paths of possible influence upon our dependent variable or variables. The kind of model testing allowed by path analysis actually encourages a more explicitly causal approach to hypothesis development than is possible with ordinary regression analysis (Asher 1976, pp. 33–36).

APPLICATION OF PATH ANALYSIS

Using Wright's rules and the path model offered in this study, an example of the application of path analysis can be examined step by step. It is hoped that this will clarify the utility of the technique and reduce the trepidation with which it is so often viewed. The arrow diagram tested in the study is reproduced below using only the variable subscripts and not the full variable names.

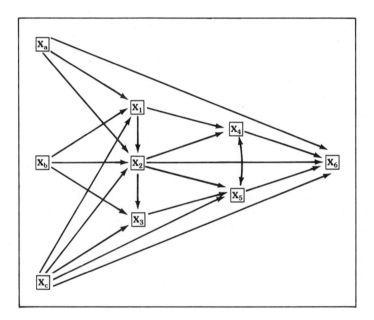

The ultimate dependent variable being measured, obviously, is x_6. To compute the influences upon x_6 (or upon any of the other intermediary variables that are dependent variables of an earlier stage of the model), both direct and indirect influences must be computed. Writing and explaining the methods of calculating all of the path equations represented in this model would be extremely lengthy and very repetitious, and an adequate illustration of path analysis technique can be achieved by utilizing one segment of the model. Path analysis will be explained with reference to the total influences represented in the model upon feminism (x_2). Thus, the portion of the model being referred to will be the following:

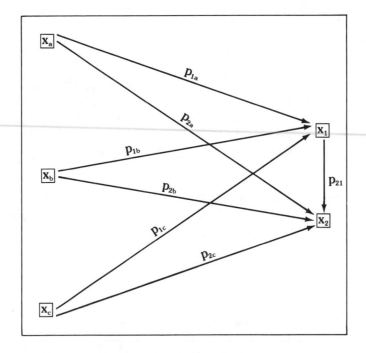

From the above path diagram, we see that seven direct paths are involved in the model: p_{1a}, p_{2a}, p_{1b}, p_{2b}, p_{1c}, p_{2c}, and p_{21}. Because of the intermediary role of variable x_1, however, three additional indirect paths are involved in any full calculation of influences upon x_2. These indirect paths represent the influence of x_a, x_b, and x_c through x_1. Direct path coefficients are simply standardized regression coefficients (betas). Thus, the path to any one variable directly from another can be represented by the beta of that regression equation. Indirect paths, as Wright's second rule indicates, are computed by generating the product of the simple or direct paths of which the indirect path is comprised. Thus, for example, when computing the influences upon feminism (x_2), the requisite equations must include all direct and indirect paths to x_2. Total effects upon x_2 involve, then, the sum of these seven path coefficients as follows:

$$x_2 = p_{2a} + p_{2b} + p_{2c} + p_{1a} p_{21} + p_{1b} p_{21} + p_{1c} p_{21}$$

The first four coefficients represent the four direct paths to variable x_2 and the latter three coefficients represent the indirect paths generated by multiplying together the direct path coefficients involved in the indirect influence of an exogenous variable upon variable x_2 through variable x_1.

Decomposing effects upon x_2 in this manner yields direct, indirect, and total effects upon the variable under study.

Formally, statements that interpret path coefficients are most helpful when they compare the relative magnitude of coefficients (paths) within the same model and the relative total effects of one variable upon another. Thus, in the illustration above, a table that decomposed effects might appear as follows:

TABLE C.1: Influences of x_a, x_b, x_c, and x_1 upon x_2

Predetermined Independent Variable	Direct Effect	Indirect Effect	Total Effects
x_a	p_{2a}	$p_{1a}\,p_{21}$	$p_{2a} + p_{1a}\,p_{21}$
x_b	p_{2b}	$p_{1b}\,p_{21}$	$p_{2b} + p_{1b}\,p_{21}$
x_c	p_{2c}	$p_{1c}\,p_{21}$	$p_{2c} + p_{1c}\,p_{21}$
x_1	p_{21}	—	p_{21}

Source: Compiled by the author.

A NOTE ON MULTICOLLINEARITY

The problem of multicollinearity leads to substantial standard errors in estimated regression coefficients. Thus, the presence of high multicollinearity reduces the accuracy of causal estimates made on the basis of standardized regression coefficients, since path estimates can differ dramatically between samples. Since multicollinearity arises from instability in sample estimates, it is most likely to be a problem with aggregate data rather than with survey (individual) data. In aggregate data, random measurement error portions of scores are likely to be canceled; in survey data, such random measurement error is always present and by the law of large numbers tends to cancel itself out. The presence of random error "attenuates correlation coefficients, thereby making the problem of collinearity less likely" (Asher 1976, p. 49).

This discussion of causal modeling and path analysis was put in the simplest of terms in hopes that any researcher with a basic familiarity with regression techniques would find the discussion comprehensible and, hence, be more attracted to than intimidated by the technique of path analysis. For the practitioner who wishes further knowledge and prefers a more technical discussion, the following works should prove helpful: Asher 1976; Blalock 1964, 1968; Goldberger 1970; Hauser and Goldberger 1971; Selltiz et al. 1959; Van Meter and Asher 1973; and Wright 1960, 1934.

BIBLIOGRAPHY

Abbott, Sidney, and Barbara Love. 1972. *Sappho was a Right-On Woman: A Liberated View of Lesbianism*. New York: Stein and Day.

Aberbach, Joel D., and Jack L. Walker. 1973. *Race in the City*. New York: Little, Brown.

——. 1970. "The Meanings of Black Power." *American Political Science Review* 64 (June):367–88.

Aberbach, Joel D. 1969. "Alienation and Political Behavior." *American Political Science Review* 63 (March):86–99.

——. 1967. *Alienation and Race*. Ph.D. dissertation, Yale University.

Abramson, Paul R. 1972. "Political Efficacy and Political Trust Among Black School Children: Two Explanations." *Journal of Politics* 34 (November):1243–77.

Adorno, Ted W., Else-Frenkel-Brunswick, Daniel V. Levinson and R. Nevitt Sanford. 1950. *The Authoritarian Personality*. New York: Harper.

Alker, H. R., Jr. 1969. "Statistics and Politics: The Need for Causal Data Analysis." In *Politics and the Social Sciences*, edited by S. M. Lipset. New York: Oxford University Press.

Allport, Gordon. 1964. *Personality and Social Encounter*. Boston: Beacon Press.

Almond, Gabriel, and Sidney Verba. 1965. *The Civic Culture*. Boston: Little, Brown.

Alwin, Duane F., and Robert M. Hauser. 1975. "The Decomposition of Effects in Path Analysis." *American Sociological Review* 49 (February):37–47.

Amundsen, Kristen. 1977. *A New Look at the Silenced Majority*. Englewood Cliffs, N.J.: Prentice-Hall.

——. 1971. *The Silenced Majority*. Englewood Cliffs, N.J.: Prentice-Hall.

Andersen, Kristi. 1975. "Working Women and Political Participation, 1952–1972." *American Journal of Political Science* 19 (August):439–54.

Angrist, Shirley. 1969. "The Study of Sex Roles," *Sex Roles* 25 (January):215–32.

Apter, David A. 1964. *Ideology and Discontent*. New York: Free Press.

Ash, Roberta. 1972. *Social Movements in America*. Chicago: Markham.

Asher, Herbert. 1976. *Causal Modeling*. Beverly Hills, Calif.: Sage.

Ashford, Douglas E. 1972. *Ideology and Participation*. Beverly Hills, Calif.: Sage.

Babcox, Deborah and Madeline Belkin (eds.). 1971. Liberation Now! *Writings from the Women's Liberation Movement*. New York: Dell.

Bardwick, Judith. 1971. *The Psychology of Women: A Study of Bio-Cultural Conflicts*. New York: Harper and Row.

Bardwick, Judith, and Elizabeth Douvan. 1971. "Ambivalence: the Socialization of Women." In *Women in Sexist Society: Studies in Power and Powerlessness*, edited by Vivian Gornick and Barbara Moran. New York: Basic Books.

Bennett, Stephen. 1973. "Consistency Among the Public's Social Welfare Attitudes in the 1960's." *American Journal of Political Science* (August):544–70.

Benston, Margaret. 1969. "The Political Economy of Women's Liberation." *Monthly Review* 24, 1:1–15.

Bertelson, Judy. 1974. "Political Interest, Influence and Inefficacy," *American Political Quarterly* 2, 4 (October):412–26.

Best, Michael H., and William E. Connolly. 1975. *The Politicized Economy.* Lexington, Mass.: D. C. Heath.

Bezdek, William, and Fred L. Strodtbeck. 1970. "Sex-Role Identification and Pragmatic Action." *American Sociological Review* 35 (June):491–502.

Biddle, Bruce J., and Edwin J. Thomas, eds. 1966. *Role Theory: Concepts and Research.* New York: Wiley.

Bien, Zeungnam, and G. R. Boynton. 1976. "Personal Problems and Public Support for the Political System: A Formalization." A paper presented at the Conference on Support for Political Institutions, May 1976, Palo Alto, Calif.

Bird, Caroline. 1968. *Born Female.* New York: David McKay.

Blalock, Hubert. 1970. *An Introduction to Social Research.* Englewood Cliffs, N.J.: Prentice Hall.

———. 1968. "Theory Building and Causal Inferences." In *Methodology in Social Research,* edited by Hubert M. Blalock and Ann B. Blalock. New York: McGraw-Hill.

———. 1964. *Causal Inferences in Nonexperimental Research.* Chapel Hill: University of North Carolina Press.

———. 1960. *Social Statistics.* New York: McGraw-Hill.

Bluhm, William T. 1974. *Ideologies and Attitudes: Modern Political Culture.* Englewood Cliffs, N.J.: Prentice Hall.

Blumer, Herbert. 1957. "Collective Behavior." In *Review of Sociology: Analysis of a Decade,* edited by Joseph B. Gittier. New York: Wiley.

———. 1951. "Social Movements." In *New Outline of the Principles of Sociology,* edited by A. M. Lee. New York: Barnes and Noble.

Boynton, G. R., Samuel C. Patterson, and Ronald D. Hedlund. 1969. "The Missing Links in Legislative Politics: Attentive Constituents." *Journal of Politics* 31 (August):700–21.

Bradburn, Norman. 1969. *The Structure of Psychological Well-Being.* Chicago: Aldine.

Brady, David W., and Kent L. Tedin. 1976. "Ladies in Pink: Religion and Political Ideology in the Anti-ERA Movement." *Social Science Quarterly* 56 (March): 564–76.

Brody, Richard, and Paul Sniderman. 1975. "Personal Problems and Public Support for the Political System." A paper presented at the Conference on Political Alienation, January 1975, Iowa City, Iowa.

Brown, Steven R. 1970. "Consistency and the Persistence of Ideology: Some Experimental Results." *Public Opinion Quarterly* 34 (Spring):60–68.

Bullock, Charles S., III, and Patricia Lee F. Hays. 1972. "Recruitment of Women for Congress: A Research Note." *Western Political Quarterly* 25 (September).

Campbell, Angus, Philip E. Converse, Warren E. Miller, and Donald E. Stokes. 1964. *The American Voter.* Ann Arbor, Michigan: University of Michigan Press.

———. 1954. *The Voter Decides.* Evanston, Ill.: Row, Peterson.

Cantril, Hadley. 1941. *The Psychology of Social Movements.* New York: Wiley.

Caplan, N. and Jeffrey Paige. 1968. "A Study of Ghetto Riots." *Scientific American* 219, 2:15–21.

Caplow, Theodore. 1975. *Toward Social Hope.* New York: Basic Books.

Carden, Maren Lockwood. 1974. *The New Feminist Movement.* New York: Russell Sage.

Chafe, William H. 1972. *The American Woman: Her Changing Social, Economic and Political Roles, 1920–1970.* Oxford: Oxford University Press.

Chafetz, Janet Saltzman. 1974. *Masculine/Feminine or Human?* Itasca, Ill.: F. E. Peacock.

Cherniss, Cary. 1972. "Personality and Ideology: A Personological Study of Women's Liberation." *Psychiatry* 35 (May):109–25.

Clarke, James W. 1973. "Race and Political Behavior." In *Comparative Studies of Blacks and Whites in the United States,* edited by Kent S. Miller and Ralph M. Dreger. New York: Seminar Press.

Cochran, Thomas C. 1972. *Social Change in Industrial Society.* London: George Allen and Unwin.

Converse, Philip. 1964. "The Nature of Belief Systems in Mass Publics." In *Ideology and Discontent,* edited by David Apter. New York: Free Press.

Cooley, Charles Horton. 1966. *Social Process.* Carbondale, Ill.: Southern Illinois University.

Davis, Jerome. 1930. *Contemporary Social Movements.* New York: Century.

de Beauvoir, Simone. 1970. *The Second Sex.* Edited and translated by H. M. Parshley. New York: Alfred A. Knopf.

Deckard, Barbara. 1975. *The Women's Movement.* New York: Harper and Row.

Dennis, Jack. 1976. "Who Supports the Presidency?" *Transaction/Society,* vol. 13 (July/August):48–53.

———. 1975. "Trends in Public Support for the American Party System." *British Journal of Political Science* (April):187–230.

———. 1966. "Support for the Party System by the Mass Public." *American Political Science Review* 60 (September):600–15.

Dolbeare, Kenneth, Patricia Dolbeare, and Murray J. Edelman. 1977. *American Politics.* 2d ed. Lexington, Mass.: D. C. Heath.

Dudar, Helen. 1971. "Women's Lib: The War on Sexism." In *The Other Half, Roads to Women's Equality,* edited by Cynthia Fuchs Epstein and William Goode. Englewood Cliffs, N.J.: Spectrum.

Dunbar, Roxanne, and Lisa Leghorn. 1970. "Female Liberation as the Basis for Social Revolution." In *Notes from the Second Year: Women's Liberation.* New York. Xeroxed. Reprinted in *Sisterhood is Powerful,* edited by Robin Morgan. New York: Vintage, 477–92.

Duncan, Otis Dudley. 1975. *Introduction to Structural Equation Models.* New York: Academic Press.

Duverger, Maurice. 1955. *The Political Role of Women.* Paris: UNESCO.

Easton, David, and Jack Dennis. 1969. *Children in the Political System.* New York: McGraw-Hill.

Edelman, Murray. 1977. *Political Language: Words that Succeed and Policies that Fail.* New York: Academic Press.

Eishtain, Jean Bethke. 1975a. "The Feminist Movement and the Question of Equality." *Polity,* 7, 4 (Summer):452–77.

———. 1975b. "Feminist Strategies for Political Change and Their Implications." Unpublished paper. University of Massachusetts, Amherst.

Etzioni, Amitai. 1972. "The Women's Movement—Tokens versus Objectives." *Saturday Review*, May 20, 1972.

———. 1966. *Studies in Social Change*. New York: Holt, Rinehart and Winston.

Etzioni, Amitai, and Etzioni, Eva. 1964. *Social Change*. New York: Basic Books.

Finifter, Ada. 1973. *Alienation and the Social System*. New York: Wiley.

———. 1970. "Dimensions of Political Alienation." *American Political Science Review* 64 (June):389–410.

Finney, John M. 1972. "Indirect Effects in Path Analysis." *Sociological Methods and Research* 1 (November):175–86.

Firestone, Shulamith. 1970. *The Dialectic of Sex*. New York: William Morrow.

Flexner, Eleanor. 1968. *A Century of Struggle: The Women's Rights Movement in the United States*. New York: Atheneum.

Flora, Cornelia B., and Naomi B. Lynn. 1974. "Women and Political Socialization: Considerations of the Impact of Motherhood." In *Women in Politics*, edited by Jane S. Jaquette. New York: Wiley.

Forward, John R., and Jay R. Williams. 1970. "Internal-External Control and Black Militancy." *Journal of Social Issues* 26:75–92.

Freeman, Jo. 1975a. *The Politics of Women's Liberation*. Chicago: Markham.

———. ed. 1975b. *Women; A Feminist Perspective*. Palo Alto, Calif.: Mayfield.

———. 1973. "The Origins of the Women's Liberation Movement." *American Journal of Society* 78 (January):792–811.

Friedan, Betty. 1963. *The Feminine Mystique*. New York: Norton.

Gamson, William A. 1971. "Political Trust and Its Ramifications." In *Social Psychology and Political Behavior*, edited by Gilbert Abcarian and John W. Soule. Columbus, Ohio: Merrill.

———. 1968. *Power and Discontent*. New York: Dorsey.

Gelb, Joyce. 1970. "Blacks, Blocs and Ballots: The Relevance of Party Politics to the Negro." In *The Politics of Social Change*, edited by Joyce Gelb and Marian Leif Palky. New York: Holt, Rinehart.

Goffman, Erving. 1961. *Encounters*. Indianapolis: Bobbs-Merrill.

Goldberger, A. S. 1970. "On Boudon's Method of Linear Causal Analysis." *American Sociological Review* 25:97–101.

Goldschmidt, Jean, Mary M. Gergen, Karen Quigley, and Kenneth J. Gergen 1974. "The Women's Liberation Movement: Attitudes and Action." *Journal of Personality* 42 (December):601–17.

Goode, William J. 1963. *World Revolution and Family Patterns*. Glencoe, Ill.: Free Press.

Gove, Walter R., and Jeannette F. Tudor. 1973. "Adult Sex Roles and Mental Illness," *American Journal of Sociology* 78, 4 (January):812–35.

Greenstein, Fred I. 1961. "Sex-Related Differences in Childhood." *Journal of Politics* (May):320–63.

———. and Michael Lerner. 1971. *A Source Book for the Study of Personality and Politics*. Chicago: Markham.

Greer, Germaine. 1970. *The Female Eunuch*. New York: McGraw-Hill.

Gurin, Gerald, Joseph Veroff, and Sheila Feld. 1960. *Americans View their Mental Health*. New York: Basic Books.

Gurin, Patricia, et al. 1969. "Internal External Control in the Motivational Dynamics of Negro Youth." *Journal of Social Issues* 25:45–71.

Gusfield, Joseph R. 1968. "Social Movements." In *International Encyclopedia of the Social Sciences*, vol. 14, ed. David L. Sills. New York: Macmillan.

Haavio-Maunila, Elina. 1972. "Sex Roles in Politics." In *Toward a Sociology of Women*, edited by Constantina Safilios-Rothschild. Lexington, Mass.: Xerox College Publishing.

Hansen, Susan, et al. 1976. "Women's Political Participation and Policy Preferences." *Social Sciences Quarterly* 56 (March):576–90.

Harris, Louis. n.d. *1972 Virginia Slims Public Opinion Poll*. #2137, n.p.

Hauser, R. M., and A. S. Goldberger. 1971. "The Treatment of Unobservable Variables in Path Analysis." In *Social Methodology*, edited by H. L. Costner. San Francisco: Jossey-Bass.

Heberle, Rudolf. 1951. *Social Movements*. New York: Appleton-Century-Crofts.

Heberle, Rudolf, and Joseph R. Gusfield. 1968. "Social Movements." In *International Encyclopedia of the Social Sciences*, vol. 14, ed. David L. Sills. New York: Macmillan.

Heiskanen, Veronica Stolte, and Elina Haavio-Maunila. 1967. "The Position of Women in Society: Formal Ideology vs. Everyday Ethic." *Social Science Information* 6:5–17.

Holter, Harriet. 1970. *Sex Roles and Social Structure*. Oslo: Universitetsforlaget.

Horney, Karen. 1973. "The Flight from Womanhood" and "The Problem of Feminine Masochism." In *Psychoanalysis and Women*, edited by Jean Baker Miller. New York: Penguin Books.

———. 1967. *Feminine Psychology*. Edited by Harold Kelman. New York: W. W. Norton.

Huber, Joan, and William H. Form. 1973. *Income and Ideology*. New York: Free Press.

Jacob, He6rbert. 1971. "Problems of Scale Equivalency in Measuring Attitudes in American Subcultures." *Social Science Quarterly* 52 (June):61–75.

Jaggar, Alison. 1977. "Political Philosophies of Women's Liberation." In *Feminism and Philosophy*, edited by Mary Vetterling-Braggin et al. Totowa, N.J.: Littlefield, Adams.

Janeway, Elizabeth. 1971. *Man's World, Woman's Place*. New York: Delta.

Jaquette, Jane S. 1974. *Women in Politics*. New York: Wiley.

Jennings, M. Kent, and Richard G. Niemi. 1971. "The Division of Political Labor Between Mothers and Fathers." *American Political Science Review* 65, 1:69–82.

Jennings, M. Kent, and Norman Thomas. 1968. "Men and Women in Party Elites: Social Roles and Political Resources." *Midwest Journal of Political Science* 12, 4:469–92.

Johnston, Jill. 1973. *Lesbian Nation: The Feminist Solution*. New York: Simon and Schuster.

Kelly, Gail Paradise. 1970. "Women's Liberation and the New Left." *Radical America* 4 (1970):19–25.

King, C. Wendell. 1956. *Social Movements in the United States*. New York: Random House.

Kish, Leslie, and Irene Hess. n.d. "The Survey Research Center's National Sample of Dwellings." Institute for Social Research, #2315. Ann Arbor, Michigan: Institute for Social Research, University of Michigan.

Knoche, Claire F. 1978. *Feminism and Political Participation: The Role of Ideology, 1972-76.* Ph.D. dissertation. Madison: University of Wisconsin.

Koedt, Anne, Ellen Levine, and Anita Rapone, eds. 1973. *Radical Feminism.* New York: Quadrangle Books.

Kontopoulos, Kyriakos M. 1972. "Women's Liberation as a Social Movement." In *Toward a Sociology of Women,* edited by Constantina Safilios-Rothschild. Lexington, Mass.: Xerox College Publishing.

Krauss, Wilma Rule. 1974. "Political Implications of Gender Roles: A Review of the Literature." *American Political Science Review* (December). 1706-23.

Kreps, Bonnie. 1973. "Radical Feminism 1." In *Radical Feminism,* edited by Anne Koedt, Ellen Levine, and Anita Rapone. New York: Quadrangle Books.

Lang, Kurt, and Gladys Lang. 1961. *Collective Dynamics.* New York: Cromwell.

Lansing, Marjorie. 1974. "The American Woman, Voter and Activist." In *Women in Politics,* edited by Jane S. Jaquette. New York: Wiley.

Lasswell, Harold. 1950. *Politics: Who Gets What, When, How?* New York: Peter Smith.

———, Nathan Leites, et al. 1949. *Language of Politics.* Cambridge, Mass.: MIT Press.

Lipsky, Michael. 1968. "Protest as a Political Resource." *American Political Science Review* 62 (December):144-58.

Litt, Edgar. 1970. *Beyond Pluralism: Ethnic Politics in America.* Glenview, Ill.: Scott, Foresman.

Lowi, Theodore. 1971. *The Politics of Disorder.* New York: Basic Books.

Lynn, Naomi, and Cornelia Flora. 1973. "Motherhood and Political Participation: The Changing Sense of Self." *Journal of Military and Political Sociology* (March):91-103.

Lynn, Naomi. 1975. "Women in American Politics: An Overview." In *Women: A Feminist Perspective,* edited by Jo Freeman. Palo Alto, Calif.: Mayfield.

Mankoff, M. 1968. "The Political Socialization of Radicals and Militants in the Wisconsin Student Movement During the '60s." Ph.D. dissertation, University of Wisconsin—Madison.

Marcus, George, David Talb, and John S. Sullivan 1974. "The Application of Individual Differences Scaling to the Measurement of Political Ideologies. *American Journal of Political Science* 18 (May):405-20.

Marcuse, Herbert. 1974. "Marxism and Feminism." *Women's Studies* 2:279-88.

McAfee, Kathy, and Myrna Wood. 1970. "Bread and Roses." In *Voices from Women's Liberation,* edited by Leslie B. Tanner. New York: Signet Books.

McLaughlin, Barry. 1969. *Studies in Social Movements.* New York: Free Press.

McWilliams, Nancy. 1974. "Contemporary Feminism, Consciousness-Raising, and Changing Views of the Political." In *Women in Politics,* edited by Jane S. Jaquette. New York: Wiley.

Merelman, Richard E. 1969. "The Development of Political Ideology: A Framework for the Analysis of Political Socialization." *American Political Science Review* 63 (September):750-67.

Miller, Arthur. 1976. "Social Denormalization and Political Trust." Paper presented at the Conference on Political Alienation and Support. May 1976, Palo Alto, Calif.

———. 1974. "Change in Political Trust: Discontent with Authorities and Economic Policies, 1972–73." Paper presented at the Annual Meeting of the American Political Science Association, August 29–September 2, 1974, Chicago, Ill.

Millett, Kate. 1973. "Sexual Politics: A Manifesto for Revolution." In *Radical Feminism*, edited by Anne Koedt et al. New York: Quadrangle Books.

———. 1970. *Sexual Politics*. New York: Doubleday.

Mitchell, Juliet. 1971. *Woman's Estate*. New York: Pantheon Books.

Moore, Barrington, Jr. 1966. *Social Origins of Dictatorship and Democracy*. Boston: Beacon Press.

Morgan, Robin, ed. 1970. *Sisterhood is Powerful*. New York: Vintage.

Muller, Edward N. 1977. "Behavioral Correlates of Political Support," *American Political Science Review* 71, 2 (June):454–92.

———. 1976. "Growth and Decline of Political Alienation." Paper presented at the Conference on Support for Political Institutions. May 27–30, 1976, Palo Alto, Calif.

Muller, Edward N., and Thomas O. Jukam. 1977. "On the Meaning of Political Support," *American Political Science Review* 71, 4 (December):1561–95.

Nie, Norman H., Sidney Verba, Rahn R. Petrocik. 1976. *The Changing American Voter*. Cambridge: Harvard University Press.

Nie, Norman, and Kristi Andersen. 1974. "Mass Belief Systems Revisited: Political Change and Attitude Structure." *Journal of Politics* 36 (August):540–91.

Nordskog, John Eric. 1954. *Contemporary Social Reform Movements*. New York: Scribner.

"NOW Bill of Rights." 1967. Reprinted in *Sisterhood is Powerful* ed. Robin Morgan. New York: Vintage. 512–14.

NOW Times. Issues from January 1974 to July 1978. Published at 425 13th Street, NW, Washington, D.C., 20004.

O'Neill, William L. 1968. "Feminism as a Radical Ideology." In *Dissent: Explorations in the History of American Radicalism*, edited by A. Young. DeKalb, Ill.: Northern Illinois University Press.

Orum, Anthony, M., Roberta S. Cohen, Sherri, Grasmuck, and Amy Orum. 1974. "Sex, Socialization and Politics." *American Sociological Review* 39 (April): 197–209.

Paige, Jeffrey M. 1971. "Political Orientation and Riot Participation." *American Sociological Review* 36 (October):810–20.

Parkin, Frank. 1972. *Class Inequality and Political Order*. New York: Praeger.

Parsons, Talcott. 1966. "A Functional Theory of Social Change." In *Studies in Social Change*, edited by Amitai Etzioni and Eva Etzioni. New York: Basic Books.

———, and Robert Bales. 1955, *Family, Socialization and Interaction*. New York: Free Press.

Pinard, Maurice. 1968. "Mass Society and Political Movements: A New Formulation." *American Journal of Sociology* 73, 6 (May):682–90.

Polk, Barbara Bovee. 1974. "Male Power and the Women's Movement." *Journal of Applied Behavioral Science* 10:413–31.

——. 1972. "Women's Liberation: Movement for Equality." In *Toward a Sociology of Women*, edited by Constantina Safilios-Rothschild. Lexington, Mass.: Xerox College Publishing.

Pomper, Gerald. 1975. *Voters' Choice*. New York: Harper and Row.

——. 1972. "From Confusion to Clarity: Issues and American Voters, 1956–1968." *American Political Science Review* 66 (June): 415–28.

Putnam, Robert D. 1973. *The Beliefs of Politicians: Ideology Conflict and Democracy*. New Haven: Yale University Press.

Pye, Lucian W., and Sidney Verba, eds. 1965. *Political Culture and Political Development*. Princeton, N.J.: Princeton University Press.

Radicalesbians. 1971. "The Women-Identified Woman." In *Liberation Now!* edited by Deborah Babcox and Madeline Belkin.

Rawls, John. 1971. *A Theory of Justice*. Cambridge: Harvard University Press.

Redstockings Manifesto. 1969. Available from Redstockings, P.O. Box 748, Stuyvesant Station, New York, N.Y. 10009. Mimeographed.

Riger, Stephanie. 1977. "Locus of Control Belief and Women's Consciousness-Raising Group Participation." Paper presented at the 85th Annual Convention of the American Psychological Association. San Francisco.

Roberts, Ron E., and Robert Marsh Kloss. 1974. *Social Movements: Between the Balcony and the Barricade*. Saint Louis: C. V. Mosby.

Rosen, B., and R. Stalling. 1971. "Political Participation as a Function of Internal-External Locus of Control." *Psychological Reports* 29:880–82.

Rossi, Alice. 1969. "Sex Equality: The Beginnings of Ideology." *The Humanist* (September/October):3–16.

Rotter, Julian B. 1966. "Generalized Expectancies for Internal vs. External Control of Reinforcements." *Psychological Monographs*, vol. 80:1–28.

Rowbotham, Sheila. 1973. *Woman's Consciousness, Man's World*. Baltimore: Penguin.

Sanger, S. P., and H. A. Alker. 1973. "Dimensions of Internal/External Locus of Control and the Women's Liberation Movement." *Journal of Social Issues* 28, 4:115–29.

Sapiro, Virginia. 1978a. "Beyond Sex: Gender Roles and the Integration of Women into Politics." Unpublished manuscript (July), University of Wisconsin—Madison.

——. 1978b. "Sex and Games: The Study of Oppression in Political Science." Paper presented at the 1978 Annual Meeting of the American Political Science Association. August 31–September 3, 1978, New York.

——. 1976. *Socialization to and from Politics: Political Gender Role Norms Among Women*. Ph.D. dissertation, University of Michigan—Ann Arbor.

Schwartz, D. C. 1973. *Political Alienation and Political Behavior*. New York: Aldine.

Sears, David O., and John B. McConahay. 1973. *The Politics of Violence*. Boston: Houghton-Mifflin.

Seese, Linda. 1969. "You've Come a Long Way, Baby." *Motive* (March-April).

Seligson, Mitchell A. 1977. "Trust, Efficacy and Modes of Political Participation." Paper presented at the Annual Meeting of the Southwestern Political Science Association. March 30–April 2, 1977, Dallas, Texas.

Selltiz, Claire, Lawrence S. Wrightsman, and Stuart W. Cook. 1959. *Research Methods in Social Relations*. New York: Holt, Rinehart and Winston.

Shils, Edward, and Harry M. Johnson. 1968. "Ideology." In *International Encyclopedia of the Social Sciences*, vol. 7, edited by David L. Sills, pp. 66–85. New York: Macmillan.

Simon, Herbert A. 1967. "Theories of Decision-Making in Economic and Behavioral Sciences." In *Surveys of Economic Theory*, vol. 3. Prepared for the American Economic Association and the Royal Economic Society. New York: St. Martin's Press.

Smelser, Niel J. 1967. "Determinants of Collective Behavior." In *Readings on Social Change*, edited by Wilbert E. Moore and Robert M. Cook. Englewood Cliffs, N.J.: Prentice-Hall.

——. 1963. *Theory of Collective Behavior*. New York: Free Press.

Smuts, Robert. 1971. *Women and Work in America*. New York: Schocken Books.

Sniderman, Paul. 1975. *Personality and Democratic Politics*. Berkeley: University of California.

Soule, John, and William McGrath. 1974. "A Comparative Study of Male-Female Political Attitudes at Citizen and Elite Levels." Paper presented at the 1974 Annual Meeting of the American Political Science Association. September 1–4, 1974, Chicago, Ill.

Steinem, Gloria. 1978. "Far from the Opposite Shore, or, How to Survive Though a Feminist." *Ms.* 7 (July):65.

Stimson, James A. 1975. "Belief Systems: Constraint, Complexity and the 1972 Election. *American Journal of Political Science*, 19, 3 (August):393–417.

Tanner, Leslie B., ed. 1970. *Voices from Women's Liberation*. New York: Signet Books.

Tatlock, John H., III, and Kent L. Tedin. 1978. "Recruitment into the Anti-ERA Movement: An Exploration into Attitudes and Motivations." Paper presented at the 1978 meeting of the Midwest Political Science Association. April 19–22, 1978, Chicago, Ill.

Thompson, Mary Lou, ed. 1970. *Voices of the New Feminism*. Boston: Beacon Press.

Toch, Hans. 1965. *The Social Psychology of Social Movements*. Indianapolis: Bobbs-Merrill.

Toffler, Alvin. 1970. *Future Shock*. New York: Bantam.

Turner, Ralph H., and Lewis M. Killian. 1957. *Collective Behavior*. Englewood Cliffs, N.J.: Prentice-Hall.

Van Meter, D. S., and Herbert B. Asher. 1973. "Causal Analysis: Its Promise for Policy Studies." *Policy Studies Journal* 2 (Winter):103–9.

Verba, Sidney, and Norman Nie. 1972. *Participation in America*. New York: Harper and Row.

Von Stein, Lorenz. 1964. *The History of the Social Movement in France, 1789–1950*. Translated by Kaethe Mangeberg. Totawa, N.J.: Bedminster Press.

Ware, Celestine. ed. 1970. "New York Radical Feminist Manifesto." In *Woman Power*. New York: Tower Public Affairs Books.

Weisberg, Herbert, and Jerrold Rusk. 1970. "Political Belief Systems and Political Behavior." *Social Science Quarterly* (December):477–93.

Weissburg, Robert. 1973. "Political Efficacy and Political Illusion." Unpublished manuscript, Cornell University.

Welch, Susan. 1977. "Women as Political Animals? A Test of Some Explanations for Male-Female Participation Differences." *American Journal of Political Science* 21, 4 (November):711–31.

———. 1973. "Support Among Women for the Issues of the Woman's Movement." *The Sociological Quarterly* 16 (Spring):216–27.

Whitehurst, Carol A. 1977. *Women in America: The Oppressed Majority.* Santa Monica, Calif.: Goodyear.

Wilker, Harry R., and Lester W. Milbrath. 1972. "Political Belief Systems and Political Behavior." In *Political Attitudes and Public Opinion,* edited by Dan D. Nimmo and Charles M. Bonjean. New York: McKay.

Yates, Gayle Graham. 1975. *What Women Want; The Ideas of the Movement.* Cambridge, Mass.: Harvard University Press.

Young, Michael, and Peter Willmott, 1973. *The Symmetrical Family.* London: Rutledge and Kegan Paul.

ABOUT THE AUTHOR

CLAIRE KNOCHE FULENWIDER is a political scientist who received her B.A. at Hood College, Frederick, Maryland, and her M.A. and Ph.D. at the University of Wisconsin-Madison, both in political science. She also earned a master's degree in education from Western Maryland College, Westminster, Maryland. She has taught at Hood College, where she is now a trustee, and at the University of Wisconsin-Madison.

Presently, Fulenwider teaches in the Women's Studies Program at the UW-Madison and is a project director for the Wisconsin Center for Public Policy where she directs a major grant for the U.S. Department of Energy conducting research on alternative energy policy. Active in the women's movement since the late '60s, Fulenwider has written various articles of a professional and general nature dealing with women, political attitudes and behavior, and energy policy.